The Nature of the Devil
AN
INQUIRY
INTO THE
Scripture Meaning of the Word

SATAN,

AND ITS

SYNONIMOUS TERMS,

The DEVIL, or the ADVERSARY, and the WICKED-ONE.

WHEREIN ALSO,
The NOTIONS concerning DEVILS, or DEMONS, are brought down to the STANDARD of SCRIPTURE.
The Whole INTERSPERSED with
REMARKS on various TERMS, PASSAGES, and PHRASES in the OLD and NEW TESTAMENTS: and undertaken with a View to illustrate the SCRIPTURES, and to separate the WORD of GOD from the DOCTRINES and TRADITIONS of MEN.

William Ashdowne
1723 - 1810

"What is written in the law? How readest thou?"
-- Luke x. 26.

ADVERTISEMENT.

CHRISTIANS, for many centuries past, have had such variable notions concerning Satan and his Power, and the present prevailing notions are so unsettled, that there is no such thing as fixing them from the writings of Divines: the Author therefore intends, in the course of this inquiry, to search the scriptures, and to fix them on that foundation, which is, indeed, by much the surest.

But the inquiry is set on foot with more views than one: for if it should detect a prevailing error, more or less supported by all systems of Divinity, it will point out the danger of an implicit Faith, and may induce many to read the Scriptures more attentively, and to give them that preference, in matters of doctrine, which is justly due to them.

Moreover, It is intended to prove, that many of the difficulties, which we meet with in the scriptures themselves, and which are so often complained of, arise from preconceived opinions, from wrong ideas annexed to scripture terms, and from mistranslations.

Lastly, It has been said, that "the Scriptures are a field for contention;" but this opinion the Author hopes to confute, by shewing that the sacred writers speak uniformly and consistently to the same point, and elucidate each other, so as to leave no just grounds for dispute and cavil. These and other good purposes may be answered by a candid inquiry; and a candid inquiry is all that is intended --for no alteration should be made in the prevailing faith, unless it should appear to be groundless, erroneous, and unsupported by scripture.

The following sheets contain only Introductory Remarks and Dissertations, with so much of the Inquiry as relates to the Old Testament: but the Remainder shall follow in due time, if the Public should seem disposed to receive it with candour. However, it is fit that the Old Testament should FIRST be thoroughly canvassed: and it is hoped, that fresh light may be thrown upon the subject, from the quarter, by such as are conversant in the Oriental Languages.

The TITLE prefixed is adapted to the whole work, which will be included in as narrow a compass as is consistent with a full inquiry: and the Author has no doubt but that the Reader will agree with him in this, viz. that the Scriptures should be handled cautiously, and that seemingly new interpretations of them should be considered leisurely.

Introductory Remarks
AND
DISSERTATIONS.

IT is well known to the learned, that language is fluctuating and variable --so much, that the same word has denoted different things, in different periods of time: this may be exemplified in the word villain, which was once the appellation of any man, however honest, who held his lands by a servile or laborious tenure; but, at this time, is applicable only to a man of vile principles or practices[1].

The word Satan may, possibly, have varied its signification: and tho' it is now said to signify a Prince, or Chief, of fallen Angels, it is not clear that this was its original acceptation: neither is it clear that any Angels ever did fall--if by Angel we are to understand a spiritual intelligent Being, as the word is usually defined.

Such a Notion, and that too with all the authority of doctrine, hath long prevailed in the Christian Church, and is grounded, chiefly, on two Texts in the New Testament: but how favourable soever our translation, and others, may be to such a notion, it is not well supported by the original: for, in the Greek, it is uncertain whether any thing be said of Angels, in the above sense of the word. The texts are capable of a very different construction, no less pertinent to the argument which they are brought to support, and appear to be references to a notable passage in the Old Testament.

The two Texts which I am speaking of, are, 2 Peter ii. 4: -- and Jude 6: we shall introduce and examine them, in their proper

---

[1] So also the word Knave was formerly used to denote a servant: and an old translation of the New Testament has "Paul a Knave of Christ."

contexts, that the reader may be able to form a more correct judgment of them.

St Peter, towards the end of the first Chapter, of this his second Epistle, commends the persons to whom he wrote, for taking heed to a more sure word of prophecy: "For (says he) prophecy came not in old time by the will of Man; but holy men of God spake as they were moved by the Holy Ghost." He then adds what, I conceive, should be translated as follows, or to the same purport.

"But there were also false Prophets among the people, as among you there will be false Teachers, who will introduce destructive heresies[2], and denying the Lord[3] that bought them, do bring upon themselves swift destruction. And many shall follow their destructive heresiesd, through whom the way of truth shall be blasphemed, and in covetousness with feigned words they will make merchandise of you: to whom the judgment of old lingereth not, and the destruction of them (of old) slumbereth not[4]. For if

---

[2] Καὶ πολλοὶ ἐξακολυθήσουσιν αὐτῶν ταῖς ἀπωλείαις. either "to their destructive heresies", the latter substantive being left out, or "to their destructions" that is, to like destructions. Οἵτινες παρεισάξυσιν αἱρέσεις ἀπωλείας

[3] Τὸν — δεσπότην See Job v. 8. Κύριον δὲ τὸν πάντων δεσπότην ἐπικαλέσομαι LXX.

[4] Οἷς τὸ κρῖμα ἔκπαλαι ὐκ ἀργεῖ, ᾗ ἡ ἀπώλεια αὐτῶν ὐ νυσάζει. Verse 3, — ἔκπαλαι Ch. iii. 5. G. Test. — " Τὸ κρῖμα ἔκπαλαι." "The judgment of old" is the same sort of expression as, " Τὸ δικαίωμα ἔμπροσθεν,, "The ordinance formerly." Ruth iv. 7. See also Zacharias iv. 4. Malachias iii. 4. LXX. The Apostle here speaks of a judgment long since past, and of a destruction which overtook certain men of old, whose case was nearly similar In our translation, "If God spared not the Angels, &c." --but the Greek Language knows no distinction between an Angel and a Messenger. I have therefore done no violence to the Original: and, it is

God spared not the Messengers that sinned, but having tartarized them with chains of darkness, delivered them, thus reserved, unto judgment[5]; and spared not the old world, but preserved Noe the eighth a preacher of righteousness, having brought a flood upon the world of the ungodly; and did reduce the Cities of Sodom and Gomorrha into ashes, condemned to that Catastrophe, being made an ensample to those who should after live ungodly ; and delivered just Lot offended with the filthy conversation of the wicked -- the Lord knoweth how to deliver the godly out of temptation, and to reserve the unjust unto the day of judgment to be punished."

This translation may be compared with our English version of the New Testament, and both of them with the original. The most material alteration is in verse the 4th, -- where, instead of the Angels, I have put the Messengers, that sinned. These Messengers, I apprehend, are no other than the men who were

---

apprehended, there are good and sufficient reasons, why we should rather prefer the word Messengers. It does not appear to me, that there was, in the apostles time, even so much as a tradition concerning Angels that had sinned; but suppose there had, we can refer to something, better than tradition, as a proof that God did not spare certain Messengers that sinned -- that they were tartarized with chains of darkness, and thus reserved unto judgment, -- to which they were at length delivered. That the Apostle here refers to a judgment past, is, I think, exceeding plain: It is apprehended his language, fairly taken, will admit of no other construction: for the participle passive, τετηρημένους which is in the perfect tense, can never be made to respect the future: and the other participles and verbs, in the aorist tense, have as certainly and evidently, a past signification in this verse, as others, in the same tense, have in the following verses. Add, to this, that the whole context of the passage requires this construction. to that of false Teachers. He proceeds to mention them in the very next verse.

[5] Εἰ γὰρ ὁ Θεὸς ἀγγέλων ἁμαρτησάντων οὐκ ἐφείσατο, ἀλλὰ σειραῖς ζόφου ταρταρώσας, παρέδωκεν εἰς κρίσιν τετηρημένους. Ver, 4.

sent, from the wilderness of Paran, to search the Land of Canaan, which the Lord had promised to the Children of Israel. They were Messengers that sinned, for when they returned, they laid before the people an evil and exaggerated report, which caused the heart of the people to faint, and discouraged them from following the Lord who had promised. It moreover appears that they: were tartarized with chains of darkness; for notwithstanding all that the Lord had done, before their eyes in the land of Egypt, and at the Red Sea -- notwithstanding he had given them Bread from Heaven, and Waters out of the stony Rock -- notwithstanding they had heard his Voice, and seen his Glory at the Mount; yet, after all this, they had not eyes to see, nor hearts to understand; but still erred and fell away in the day of temptation[6]: the Light

---

[6] The history of these Messengers, referred to by the Apostle, is to be found in the xiii. and xiv. Chapters of the Book of Numbers. See also Chap. xxxii. 8, 9, and Deut, i. 28. -- from whence it appears, that the great apostacy from the Lord, in the wilderness, is imputed to these Messengers, who brought up an evil report upon the Land, and persuaded the people, that unsurmountable difficulties stood between them and the possession of it. There was, indeed, an evil heart of unbelief among the people; but, considering the station of the Messengers, they were most guilty: hence a more speedy and severe judgment overtook them. Caleb and Joshua, were not of the number of them that sinned: these two Messengers wholly followed the Lord, and stood forth, with Moses and Aaron, to stem the defection of the people, assuring them that they would be well able, since the Lord was with them, to surmount all obstacles -- only, added they, ἀπὸ τῦ κυρίυ μὴ ἀποϛάτα γίνεϑε -- "be not ye apostates from the Lord" -- but the Evil Report of their Brethren prevailed. Of these it may well be said that they were, σειραῖς ζόφυ ταρταρώσας -- "tartarized with chains of darkness." If their case be attentively considered, this expression will not be thought too strong. It is said of the Egyptians that they were δέσμιοι σκότυς ἢ μακρᾶς πέδηϛαι νυκτὸς "bound of darkness and fettered of long night." -- Vide, LXX. Wisdom of Sol. xvii. 2. -- but these Messengers appear to have been under a worse than Egyptian darkness: and it was with them, as it was afterwards, with other Rulers of this stubborn People, they were, in the

had shined unto them, but they loved darkness rather: and from their whole conduct, we may infer, that as they justly might so they really were judicially blinded in the end: or, as the Apostle expresses it, guarded or reserved under chains of darkness unto judgment -- to which they were at length delivered: for those Men " Even those Men, that did bring up the evil report upon the Land, died by the plague before the Lord⁷."

---

end, judicially blinded. I understand the word, ταρ]αρώσας "tartarized," to be expressive of the gloomy horrors of their own minds: they shrunk at every difficulty, were always desponding, and never saw anything, before their eyes, but destruction and death; whereas faith, as a grain of Mustard Seed, would have filled them with the most lively hope, and have been an anchor to their Souls. Modern unbelievers might learn from these, their brethren of old, to retreat in time, left their bands be made strong -- lest chains of darkness be judicially laid on. Like modes of expression occur -- Psalm cvii. 10. Καθημένυς ἐν σκότει ἢ σκιᾷ θανάτυ, πεπεδημένυς ἐν πτωχείᾳ ἢ σιδήρῳ "Sitting in darkness and in the Shadow "of Death, enchained in Poverty and Iron." And Proverbs v. 22. σειραῖς δὲ τῶν ἑαυτῦ ἁμαρτιῶν ἕκαστος σφίγγεται, "Each bound with Chains of his own Sins."

⁷ See Numb. xiv. 37. It is apprehended this is the very judgment referred to, by the Apostle, and that he has not alluded to a future judgment: for not only the language militates against this supposition; but the context and argument do the same. How could a reference to a judgment yet future, prove that false teachers would bring a swift destruction upon themselves? If we suppose the Apostle, as our Translators have done, to have spoken of Angels that sinned, such a reference could have no weight, in his argument, any further than their judgment is allowed to have taken place. Temporal judgments only can be brought forth as Examples: and to speak of a future one here, would be, at least, superfluous to the argument. But supposing a dispute between God and his Angels, How came Men by the fact? It could not be visible; and it is not revealed. And, why should we recur to judgments both unrevealed and invisible? Is it not better to rely on known facts? we conclude then that the judgment here spoken of, is a past temporal judgment, well attested -- and is referred to by way of

We have now seen how, and in what sense, the language of the Apostle, is applicable to the Messengers. Let us just see, how such a reference, will suit with the connexion and the Apostle's argument. The passage begins with this observation -- "But there were false prophets among the people, as among you there will be false teachers," and it is afterwards added "to whom the judgment of old lingereth not, and the destruction of them" (that is, I suppose, of the false prophets of old) "slumbereth not."

Now we know that the Messengers, who went to search the land of Canaan, were all of them Heads and Rulers in their respective tribes[8]: and it is not improbable, that they were of the seventy, who were appointed to bear the burthen of the people, together with Moses -- who were once partakers of the same Spirit and prophesied[9]; but not to insist upon this, there is so much of the prophetic character upon them, and the word Prophet is used with so much latitude in the sacred writings, that we need not scruple to allow them the Title. They were sent forth by the commandment of the Lord, and the end of their being sent was, that they might bring back a faithful message. They were the Messengers of the Lord, (as all his Prophets since) and were to declare to others, that which the Lord had intrusted to them: and tho' the matter they were charged with, was not a matter of Revelation to them, yet they were prophets unto the people. Moreover, as they brought up an evil report upon the land, and added the comment of an unbelieving heart, saying, "We are not able to go up, &c." -- and as they did hereby seduce, and turn

---

ensample, along with the judgment of the Old World, of Sodom and Gomorrha, on all of whom swift destruction once came.

[8] Numb. xiii. 3. Πάντες ἄνδρες ἀρχηγοὶ υἱῶν Ἰσραὴλ ὗτοι

[9] Numb. xi. 25. I apprehend it cannot be proved either that the Messengers were of the number of the seventy, or that they were not: However Joshua, who was one of the Messengers, and afterwards led the people into the promised land, was already one of the first Men in Israel, and a chosen Man with Moses. This may seem to favour the supposition that he was of the seventy; but we leave this matter as not thinking it any ways necessary to be insisted on.

away the people, from following the Lord, they were false prophets: they stand at the head of them, and were figures or types of those who should come after.

And there is a strong appearance that the Apostle has considered them as types, and prophesied from them, of those who should come after. "There were (says he) false prophets among the people, as there will be false teachers among you." As it once was so it will be again: the former figure out the latter [10]

Certain it is, that the Messengers, did "introduce a most destructive heresy" among the people of old: for only Caleb and Joshua wholly followed the Lord, and taught the people to trust in him: they only considered him as true to his Promise, and as present with his people to subdue their Enemies, that they might inherit that Promise: the other Messengers had made ship-wreck of their Faith -- held a contrary opinion, and said we are not able to go up, the people are stronger than we: now if thus to apostatize from the Lord, to hold an opinion repugnant to his word[11], to enforce that opinion, and thereby to subvert many -- If this, I say, be not Heresy, what is? These Messengers also, "denied the Lord that bought them" -- that redeemed them from the land of Egypt: and hereby "they brought upon themselves swift destruction". Again, "many followed their destructive heresy" ---to their destruction.---And "thro' them the way of truth[12] was blasphemed:" for Moses was aware, that it would be said, "Because the Lord was not able to bring this people into the

---

[10] It is not clear that these words -- ὑπόδειγμα μελλόντων ἀσεβεῖν -- (which may be rendered "An ensample of those who shall after live ungodly,") do not refer back to the Messengers and old world, as well as to Sodom and Gomorrha. It will, at least, be allowed that the former, were as much patterns or ensamples, as the latter: and it seems as if they had been all more or less copied.

[11] It rendered the promise of God of no effect: they must go up, in order to inherit the promise.

[12] The God of Truth -- his word, worship and service, See Numb, xiv. 13. to 17.

Land which he sware unto them, therefore he hath slain them in the Wilderness."

We see then, that the character of the Messengers, as delivered down by Moses, perfectly agrees with the character of the false Teachers, as described by the Apostle: and so strong is the resemblance, that there is great reason to think, he had his eye upon the former when he described the latter. There is not indeed one new feature, unless it can be found in the following words -- "In covetousness, with feigned words, they will make merchandise of you." The Messengers dealt in feigned words; but how far they hoped to make a gain of the people I will not say[13].

From what has been said, it plainly appears, that the Messengers that sinned[14], is a reference well adapted to the Apostles purpose, and argument: and we shall not easily find another that would have suited so well: the time when these Messengers sinned -- the effect of their Apostacy -- the numbers seduced by them -- and the swift destruction which overtook them, from the Lord, made their ensample such, as might be urged, with peculiar fitness, at the beginning of the Christian Dispensation: it has its use at all times: and the wise and prudent will ever look back to it with godly fear.

The Sin, Judgment, and Destruction, of these Messengers, are attested and delivered down by Moses, faithful in the House of God, and an Eye-witness of the Facts. The whole of the matter, therefore, would be received, by Christians, as sacred and sealed truth -- was most certainly believed among them, and received under this persuasion, that it was written for their instruction: perfectly adapted to the Apostle's purpose and argument, and so

---

[13] In this, perhaps, the false teachers might bear a greater resemblance to the mercenary disposition of the old world, or of Sodom and Gomorrha, who are also referred to; but if it was a peculiarity, it was fit to be taken notice of: and it is now no new thing.

[14] St Peter here calls the Messengers that sinned οἱ ἄγγελοι ἁμαρτήσαντες The Author of the Epistle to the Hebrews, calls the People simply οἱ ἁμαρτήσαντες. Heb. iii. 17.

powerfully recommended -- where is the other instance that would have an equal effect? The Story of Angels that sinned, had it been as much believed in the apostle's time as it now is, is scarcely applicable, and could not have produced an equal effect. There is, therefore, reason to conclude, that the Apostle spake of the Messengers that sinned: and that all the instances, of the righteous judgment of God, referred to by him, are taken from the Scripture.

WE turn now to the Epistle of Jude, verse 6th which, along with its context, may be translated as follows. "Beloved I have given all diligence to write unto you of the common Salvation, it being needful to write to you, beseeching you to contend earnestly for the faith once delivered to the Saints. For certain men have crept in unawares who were of old prefigured unto this condemnation[15], ungodly (men) turning the grace of our God into lasciviousness; and denying the only Lord (δεσπότην) God

---

[15] Jude, ver. 4. -- Οἱ πάλαι προγεγραμμένοι εἰς τοῦτο τὸ κρῖμα "They of old prefigured unto this condemnation," the word prefigared is most suitable to the context, or sense of the passage at large, for the apostle has referred to the Types. The word προγεγραμμένοι (in Latin, prius descripti or coram depicti) is literally pre-described or pre-depicted; but to pre-describe any man, or set of men, in the persons of others (as in the persons of the People and Messengers in the wilderness) or to pre-depict, is exactly the same with pre-figuration. It will be said perhaps that the word sometimes signifies prescribed, in such a sense as implies ordinance: suppose it does, yet still it is a written ordinance, and this will refer us back to the Scriptures of the Old Testament: we say then that these "Certain men "crept in unawares" were no otherwise ordained unto the condemnation spoken of, than as they were prefigured in the persons of the Messengers, or of the People in the wilderness, under a former dispensation: and St Paul considers that dispensation as typical as well as St Peter and St Jude. See the Gr. Test. I Cor. x. 1st to 13th verse, and particularly the 6th and 11th verses.

and our Lord (κυριον) Jesus Christ. I will therefore put you in mind, though ye once knew this, that the Lord having saved the people out of the Land of Egypt, afterwards destroyed them that believed not. And the Messengers who watched not duly over their principality, but deserted their proper station, he kept with perpetual chains under darkness unto the judgment of the great day[16]. As also Sodom and Gomorrha, and the cities about them, who after their manner, committed fornication and followed after strange flesh, are set forth for an ensample, sustaining the judgment of eternal Fire."

This translation is, at least, as conformable to the original as that in our English Version: and I think it is less exceptionable in its sense.

By certain men crept in unawares, ungodly men, turning the grace of God into lasciviousness, and denying the only Despot, God and our Lord Jesus Christ, we are chiefly to understand false teachers, who were active in the business; but the Apostle has an eye to the deceived, as well as the deceivers: for it was his care for

---

[16] Jude 6th. Ἀγγέλους τε τοὺς μὴ τηρήσαντας τὴν ἑαυτῶν ἀρχὴν, ἀλλὰ ἀπολιπόντας τὸ ἴδιον οἰκητήριον, εἰς κρίσιν μεγάλης ἡμέρας, δεσμοῖς ἀϊδίοις ὑπὸ ζόφον τετήρηκεν. Literally translated thus "And the Messengers -- those who guarded not their Principality, but deserted their proper station, he guarded with perpetual chains under darkness, unto the judgment of the great day." The above translation is in sense the same with this: for to guard a thing is to watch duly over it, or to look well after it, but this the Messengers (who were Rulers in their respective tribes) did not do by their charge -- by which I would be understood to mean, "the people committed to their care," over whom they had τὴν ἀρχὴν -- principality; but if they exercised their authority, it was in a way directly contrary to the end for which it was given, for they perverted the people from following the Lord: therefore the Lord guarded them, or kept them duly, with perpetual chains of darkness, until that aweful day in which he thought fit to pronounce and execute his righteous judgment upon them. See Numb. xiv. 22, 23 -- and 35, 36, 37.

the people that made him give all diligence to write: and not only the deceivers, but the deceived also, were prefigured of old, unto righteous judgment or condemnation.

Therefore, Jude, who wrote with an earnest Zeal to preserve the People from seduction, sets out very judiciously, with holding up to their view the people in the wilderness who were seduced by the Messengers. He says, "I will therefore put YOU -- (that is, YOU PEOPLE) in mind, tho' ye once knew this, that the Lord having saved THE PEOPLE of old, out of the Land of Egypt, afterwards destroyed them that believed not." Nor did they -- much less did they escape, who taught or confirmed them in their unbelief: for "The Messengers, those, at least, who watched not duly over their Principality, but deserted their proper station, he kept with perpetual chains under darkness unto the Judgment of the great day." This will not need much explanation, to such as have made themselves masters of the history of the Messengers, and have attended to the remarks we have made in the foregoing pages: these Messengers had each of them a Principality -- were all of them Heads and Rulers in their respective Tribes: in this exalted station, the Lord -- the God of Abraham their Father, had placed them, that, in the Faith of HIM, they might go up at the head of HIS PEOPLE, and conduct them unto the possession of the promised land: but they watched not duly over their principality -- over those who were under their authority: they were not active, nor anxious, to keep them in the right way, -- steadfast unto the Lord: neither did they encourage, and conduct them forward, to the promised Possession: nay, they actually deserted their proper station; for they absolutely refused to go up at the head of their respective people, as was their office and duty to have done. St Jude says they were "kept with perpetual chains under darkness[17]; unto the judgment of the great day." -- So

---

[17] Δεσμοῖς ἀϊδίοις ὑπὸ ζόφον τετηρηκεν -- "he kept (or guarded) with perpetual chains under darkness" -- here is no mention of any place of darkness; but only under darkness: so, I apprehend, Peters expression σειραῖς ζόφου, ταρταρώσας which I have translated, "tartarized with

indeed it appears: otherwise they would have been enlightened, and have perceived that God was well able to bring his people into the land which he had promised, and to subdue all their Enemies under them. But let the justice of God stand clear -- they were not concluded under darkness, till they had first resisted, or closed their eyes upon, a light, which would probably have saved Sodom and Gomorrha: they were still the children of unbelief, after all his works and wonders which he had shewn them -- after all the marvellous things that he did before them, in the land of Egypt, in the field of Zoan -- after he divided the Red Sea, thro' which they passed as on dry land -- after he had "dashed in pieces" their old Enemy and Oppressor, Pharaoh, with all his chariots and his host, over whom he, the Lord, triumphed gloriously, and threw the horse and his rider into the sea. After all this these Messengers were in darkness[18] -- this ten times, saith

---

chains of darkness," is expressive only of that gloom or darkness in which their minds were held. As the apostles may be supposed, to have expressed the same thing in different words, the reader will do well to recollect, what has been obseved, on the words of St Peter.

[18] It was revealed unto Abraham, that "his seed should be strangers in a land that should afflict them 400 years -- and afterwards that nation will I judge saith the Lord." Gen. xv. 13, 14. So the Egyptians "afflicted Israel -- made them serve with rigour -- made their lives bitter with hard bondage -- slew their male children -- and mightily oppressed them." Therefore did the Lord judge that nation. "The Children of Israel sighed and their cry came up unto God -- he heard their groaning and remembered his covenant with Abraham:" here is the primary cause of the judgments upon Pharaoh and the land of Egypt. And if the Lord hardned the Hearts of Pharaoh and his People, who had before approved themselves oppressors and murtherers, ripe for destruction -- "That he might multiply his signs and his wonders, and make his name glorious throughout the earth" -- where is the injustice? The cause of the judgments existed before God spake unto Moses, and Pharaoh's heart being hardned, only determined the mode, in which they should be introduced: and nothing could be more beneficial to the world than Pharaoh's hardness. Observe also, with respect to the Messengers, that the arm of the Lord had been amply revealed, before the day in which

the Lord, have they tempted -- have they provoked me. In short their darkness was perpetual and accompanied them unto the judgment of the great day, when the Lord pronounced judgment against them, and they died of the plague before him[19]. Now if the case of the Messengers was such as has been represented, (and it is submitted to the reader whether it was not,) then, what could tend more to preserve the people of God from false teachers, than an apprehension that they were typified or prefigured under these

---

they first set foot in the wilderness -- or at least on that day: and both they and the people had already sufficient grounds for believing the Lord and trusting in his Power: certain it is, that when they had corrupted themselves with the molten calf, he threatned to consume them; what shall we say then? was not his anger justly kindled? had they not already deserved to die the death? doubtless. But suppose he forbare and suffered their manners, yet a long time in the wilderness, and kept them in chains of darkness till a future day, that he might more effectally instruct the world in his fear -- suppose this, and the dispensation is gracious. By wisely timing the judgment of these Messengers, we are taught the danger of departing from the Lord, of distrusting his Power, and of seducing his People.

[19] Εἰς κρίσιν μεγάλης ἡμέρας -- τετήρηκεν "kept them -- unto the judgment of the great day;" In Peter's Epistle -- παρέδωκεν εἰς κρίσιν τετηρημένους -- "delivered them kept or reserved unto judgment." The language, context and argument, require both to be interpreted of a judgment past: and tho' the phrases, ἡ ἡμέρα ἐκείνη, ἡ ἡμέρα κυρίου, ἡ ἡμέρα μεγάλη, &c. have mostly been understood of one day, in which God will judge the quick and dead; yet this does not always hold in the New Test. and seldom, if ever in the Old. The judgment pronounced and executed, from thenceforth upon the people, and speedily upon the Messengers, in the wilderness, signalized that day or time: hence it is called, ἡ ἡμέρα μεγάλη "the great day." It was also a day or time of Judgment: and other times of temporal judgment are still more emphatically marked. See Joel ii. 31. Malachi iv. 5. Matthew x. 23. &c.

Messengers? -- every part of whose character, as drawn out by the Apostles, is calculated to create a godly jealousy and fear: and the swift destruction which overtook them, in the day that the Lord rose up to judgment, together with the overthrow of all the People in the wilderness, who were joined to them, could not fail of having a powerful effect upon such as feared God.

WE have now examined the Texts separately: and may observe that Peter and Jude have, upon the whole, said the same things -- nearly in the same language; but there is some difference between them, which deserves to be taken notice of.

St Peter prophesied -- foretold the Brethren, that as there had been false prophets among the people of old, so there should be false teachers among them -- who would introduce destructive heresies, and deny the Lord that bought them.

St Jude did not prophesie: he had facts before him: certain men were crept in unawares, ungodly men, who were actually turning the grace of God into lasciviousness, and denying the only Lord God and our Lord Jesus Christ. So far Peter's prediction was already fulfilled.

Peter had said, respecting these men -- that many would follow their destructive heresies -- that thro' them the way of truth would be blasphemed -- and that in covetousness, with feigned words, they would make merchandise of the People.

Jude seems to have apprehended all this, and therefore, to prevent the mischief, gave all diligence to write unto the people -- referring to events recorded in the Old Test. full to the above purpose -- if considered as Types.

Peter says, that these false teachers would bring upon themselves swift destruction -- that to them the judgment of old lingered not, and the destruction of them (of old) slumbered not: this he explains and exemplifies -- by the Messengers that sinned in the wilderness, as being indeed a most applicable instance -- and supports it with two others, the old world, and Sodom and Gomorrha--on all of whom swift destruction once came.

Jude says they were prefigured, or pre-depicted of old, and barely refers the people to their types, or exemplars, THE MESSENGERS -- and herein he leaves his readers to judge of the event[20].

But what is most worthy of note, is that the two Apostles had somewhat different views in writing -- not so much upon the whole, as in those particular parts of their Epistles, which have fallen under our notice.

Peter prophesied of false teachers, and described their character, that they might be known, when they should appear. Jude had perceived their entrance into the Church, and gave all diligence to write, that he might, if possible, preserve the people from seduction. -- Hence, he very prudently confounds the false teachers, with those taught by them -- considers them together as one body of ungodly men prefigured of old -- and inserts, what it nearly concerned the People to know and keep in mind, viz. "That the Lord having saved the people out of the Land of Egypt, afterward destroyed them that believed not." And the Messengers also -- he reserved unto judgment. This was bringing the matter home to the people, and was well calculated to convince them, that their first care ought to be for themselves. And tho' this, respecting the people in the wilderness, is left out of Peter's prophecy, respecting false teachers; yet it neither is, nor

---

[20] Verse 5th, "I will therefore put you in remembrance tho' ye once knew this" -- tho' ye must have heard or read of it "how that the Lord, &c." His barely putting them in remembrance of the scriptures referred to, is, I think, a sufficient proof that he would have them considered as typical: indeed if it were not so, if God's former dispensations were not predescriptive, and certain indications, of his future dealings with men, there could be no certain instruction derived from them. This will be allowed with respect to his judgments: and similar judgments seem to imply a similarity of Character, in the persons judged.

ought to be omitted, in an address to the people to guard against them[21].

UPON the whole, nothing can be more evident, than that the persons who sinned, mentioned by St Peter, and those who watched not duly over their principalities, mentioned by St Jude, are the same; and we conclude, from the foregoing observations, that they were just as much Angels -- as those received by Rahab, the harlot; who, we certainly know, were neither more nor less than Messengers[22]. This interpretation is not only more countenanced by the language of the Apostles -- is not only more suitable to the connection and argument; but it rests on a much better foundation, on a more clear and undoubted authority, than that which is commonly received.

St Jude says, he put the people in mind of what they once knew; but supposing him to speak of "Angels which kept not their first estate; but left their own habitation, and are reserved in everlasting chains under darkness unto the judgment of a great day, yet future," as in our translation -- supposing Jude to speak thus, and whence should the people once have known it? The Old Testament says not a word of any such thing: and the whole sect of the Sadducees, in our Saviour's time, believed neither Angel nor Spirit to exist; but confined their Faith to one God only: --

---

[21] Peter refers to the Messengers only; because such reference only was full and direct to the purpose of his Prophecy respecting false teachers, who in Station and Character would resemble the Messengers; but Jude first refers to the People seduced by them, as a thing most necessary to be kept in mind, by the then People of God, when false teachers were among them. It appears to me, that Peter has prophesied from the Messengers as Types, and that Jude refers to Them and the People of old as such -- as St Paul has done in his I Epistle to the Corinthians, Chap. x..----But supposing this was not so, that would not prove that there is any reference to Angels or spiritual Beings.

[22] James ii. 25. "Was not Rahab the Harlot justified by works when she had received τὺς ἀγγέλυς, the Messengers"--sent by Joshua to spy secretly, and to view the Land, even Jericho. Joshua, Chap. ii.

apprehending, I suppose, that the Angels and Spirits, mentioned in the Old Testament, were meer imaginary Beings, introduced for the sake of representation. The Pharisees, it is true, confessed both Angels and Spirits: and the scriptures, doubtless, countenance such a belief; but as we are cautioned not to intrude into things not seen, and told that secret things belong to the Lord, we shall do well not to be wise above the reach of reason and sense, and what is written or revealed. What can fairly be collected from the scriptures, on this head, is, in sum, nearly as follows. Angels are represented unto us as a superior order of Beings, employed as the Messengers of God: and hence they derived their name. The Old and New Testaments both favour the Idea of a local Heaven, where God is more peculiarly present, where the Angels behold his face, and receive his commands: from hence they are said to be dispatched, on some particular occasions, to reveal or to execute the will of God: and once in the Old Testament we read, that God sent evil Angels among the Egyptians -- as also of the destroying angel; but this is spoken only in respect of their commission, which was to hurt and destroy; for both were perfectly subject and obedient unto God[23]: so that, on the whole, there is not the least ground to believe, that any Angel, or Angels, were supposed to have fallen, from their original dignity and allegiance to God. The Jews who confessed Spirits, considered them, chiefly, as having their place upon earth, tho' they did acknowledge others elsewhere: in the New Test. in particular, we have often read of Dæmons, of impure or evil Spirits: -- these they apprehended to be the souls of dead or

---

[23] Evil Angels, so called, because sent to inflict Plagues upon Egypt, or the Egyptians. Ps. lxxviii. 49. A destroying Angel because sent to destroy the people, or to smite with the pestilence, 2 Sam. xxiv. 16. But there are some able interpreters who think these Angels denote the plagues only: God is represented as acting by Angels or Messengers: and it is certain that "Fire and Hail, Storm and Tempest, Plague and Pestilence, may be his Messengers to fulfil his word." An appearance, in case of Plague, may denote only the divine presence: and prove, that it was from, or of the Lord, not natural.

departed men, as we shall, hereafter endeavour to prove[24]: but it doth not at all appear, that before, at, or shortly after our Saviour's time, any spirits were judged to be fallen Angels, or spiritual Existences that had sinned: both sacred and profane history give a very different account of them.

The Gods, Demi-gods, Dæmons, &c. of the Gentile world, were, indeed, very numerous; but there is nothing in the Theology, or Pneumatology, of the Heathen Writers, not even of their Poets, from whence we may conclude, that they conceived of any of them as fallen Angels: for the famous Pluto, was own brother to Jupiter, and his Ministers, tho' said to execute severe punishments, were faithful in their respective trusts, and executed judgment and justice only: -- unless the Judges erred through ignorance; tho' that was never suspected by the ancients.

Therefore whether St Jude wrote to Jews or Gentiles, there is little ground to think, that he reminded the people only of what they once knew, if he meant to be understood as speaking of Angels, or Spiritual Beings, "who kept not their first Estate, but left their own Habitation, &c"[25]. -- However, suppose we should, without reason, (or against all the reasons that have been —

---

[24] The Notions concerning Dæmons, about our Saviour's time, have been collected, from the best authorities, by Dr Lardner, in his Tracts; by Dr Newton, in his Dissertations on Prophecy; and lately by Mr Farmer, in his Dissertations on Miracles: It only remains, that we should search the Scriptures, and point out some Errors in the application of known Truths.

[25] The authority of this Epistle of Jude, as well as of the 2. Epistle of Peter, was much questioned, in the early ages of the Church, chiefly on account of some references, thought to be apocryphal: I might therefore argue, that so far as the doctrine of fallen Angels, is grounded on any thing, contained in these two epistles, so far that doctrine is of doubtful authority: and indeed if the reference to angels that sinned, were a reference to an apocryphal Book, the argument would be good. But I have not availed myself of such an argument. The prophecy of Peter, it seems, approved itself by facts: and, whenever that happened, the Epistle of Jude was worthy of acceptation.

advanced) grant that such a notion did once prevail; yet if it was merely conjecture, and rested only on human authority, is it likely, that Peter and Jude, should both put their apostolic seals to it? Or suppose we should descend a little further, and even allow the thing to have been most certainly believed, and that too upon good authority, tho' this doth not at all appear; yet still, Angels that sinned, would be an instance less adapted, to the Apostles argument, than that of the Messengers that sinned: for, besides what has already been urged on that head, we may yet add -- that if Angels and Men, have different natures and different powers (as is generally believed) then the just judgment of God upon the former, might not at all affect the latter: nor doth it appear that there is any similarity, between the circumstances of the false teachers, who should afterwards come, and the circumstances of the Angels who are said to have sinned: and if we take the passages, as they stand, in the received translation, we shall find a difference and disproportion, between the parts which ought to agree, on which account the argument becomes loose and inconclusive. We therefore conclude, that the Messengers, who by a false and evil report, caused the people of old to apostatize from the Lord, and who did thereby bring swift destruction upon themselves -- this, I say, is a reference much more applicable and proper in the case of false teachers -- against which the Apostles are cautioning the people, and shewing them that they should bear their judgment, whoever they were, as others before them had done.

But there is great reason to believe, that the notion of fallen Angels, first arose, from a misconstruction of the very passages we have been considering. The Gentiles, when they came to preach the Gospel, not being sufficiently read and skilled in the Jewish Scriptures, that is, in the Old Testament, might easily overlook the reference, and lay hold of the Texts in question to account for the Evil Spirits, mentioned in both the Old and New Testaments -- and for the Devil and his Angels, mentioned in the Gospel of Matthew. And when once these Texts came to be misconstrued of fallen angels, and that interpretation came to be received, it is no more to be wondered at, that it hath continued a received doctrine, than that the doctrines of purgatory, transubstantiation, and others, should still continue, and be received, in the Church of Rome. When error is once substituted and established for truth, it is afterwards taken for granted, without examination: so the system of fallen Angels, once wrought up, and glossed over, hath for ages been swallowed without ceremony.

But it will certainly be granted, that Peter and Jude, may have referred to the Messengers that sinned: and it ought to be granted that the Greek is not wrested, nor the sense of the passages injured, when made favourable to such a reference: hence it will follow, that all that has been said, and written, for centuries past, concerning fallen Angels, may have no grounds in Scripture: for the two passages we have been considering, have ever been urged, as the most direct proofs, that Angels did sin and fall.

There is reason, therefore, to stand in doubt whether Satan be a fallen Angel: and upon the supposition that he may not, it is proposed to search the Scriptures: a close attention to what is written therein concerning him, will, most probably, lead us to the true Idea, which we ought to annex to that formidable name.

AN INQUIRY
Into the Scripture Meaning of the Word
SATAN, &c.

THE purport of this inquiry is, chiefly, to investigate the sense of the word Satan, as it is used in sacred writ: And that we may not, at last, fix on an erroneous sense, it is proposed to examine every passage wherein the word occurs. It will be much if the spirit of God (even in this matter) has not conveyed a clear and determinate sense to posterity: Some passage or other will doubtless speak plain; and, I hope, there are none which are cloathed with impenetrable darkness. Trusting, therefore, that God has not left us in the dark, in matters which we are concerned to know and understand, we turn to his word with the greater alacrity--in humble confidence that this our labour will not be in vain. It will be proper that we should begin with the Old Testament--herein, in our English version at least, the word occurs only four times,--or on four different occasions. Namely, In the first Book of Chronicles, Chap. xxi.-- In the Book of Job, Chap. i. and ii.-- In the cixth Psalm.--And in the Prophecy of Zechariah, Chap. iii. We now proceed to examine the passages, in order as they occur, more particularly with a view to determine the sense of the word Satan. In I Chron. xxi. I. it is written that "Satan stood up against Israel, and provoked David to number Israel." We have a parallel to this scripture. 2 Samuel. Chap. xxiv. I.--where we read that "The anger of THE LORD was kindled against Israel, and HE moved David against them, to say, go number Israel and Judah."

In order to a right understanding of the History, contained in the two Chapters just referred to, and to prove that the writers of them are no ways inconsistent with each other, it may be proper to make some remarks, not absolutely necessary to the inquiry we set out upon. It has been asked, how David sinned in numbering the people? -- and, why the destroying Angel was sent forth on that occasion? In answer to these questions, we may refer to Exodus, Chap. xxx. 11th to 17th Verse -- where we are informed, that -- "The Lord spake unto Moses, saying, when thou takest the sum of the Children of Israel, after their number; then shall they give every man a ransom for his soul unto the Lord, that there be no plague among them when thou numberest them -- and thou shalt take the atonement money (which was half a shekel per man) of the Children of Israel, and shall appoint it for the service of the tabernacle of the congregation, that it may be for a memorial unto the Children of Israel before the Lord, to make an atonement for your souls." This, it seems, was to be a standing ordinance in Israel, when the sum of the people, from twenty years old and upwards, should be taken: but after such an ordinance was given, nothing but a command from God, or a strong and manifest necessity, could justify such a step as that of numbering the people: for as every man, from the richest down to the poorest, was to give half a shekel on this occasion, David ought not to have amused himself, at such an expence to each individual in his kingdom, who exceeded the age of twenty years: and to number the people without the ransom was a direct transgression of the ordinance. This without all doubt was the real truth of the matter: David appears to have had no intention of taking the ransom money of the people, when he sent Joab to number them; but only to know their number. In this, therefore, he sinned against an ordinance of the Lord, and the ransom not being given by the people, was the apparent trespass for which they fell. The King's order to number the people was disagreeable (the text says abominable) to Joab: and he expostulated with his Uncle, saying, "Why doth my Lord require this thing? Why will he be a cause of trespass to Israel?" He, and the Captains of the host, considered the matter as drawing the whole nation into a trespass: Notwithstanding they could not prevail with David to desist. Such was his curiosity to know the number of the people! As the history in Samuel is first, in the order of our Bible, and traces the matter to the fountain, we shall clear it, in the first place, and then proceed to shew, how the account in the Chronicles is perfectly consistent and reconcileable therewith. In Samuel it is faid -- "Again the anger of the Lord was kindled against Israel, and he moved David against them, to say, go number Israel and Judah." The same form of expression occurs frequently in the Old Testament. It is said that "God moved the Captains of the King of Syria, to depart from Jehoshaphat King of Judah[26]:" And David said unto Saul "If the Lord have stirred thee up (or, have moved thee[27]) against me, let him accept an offering; but if the children of men, cursed be they before the Lord." The Lord, also, is said, -- to move to jealousy, -- to stir up adversaries, -- to stir up a scourge, -- to stir up the Medes, &c. There is, no doubt, a propriety in this mode of expression: it denotes that the providence of God, is some way concerned, in bringing about those things, unto which he is said to move; or that such and such movements are by his appointment. To the same effect, Adonijah says "The Kingdom is turned about, and is become my brother's, for it was his from the Lord[28]." -- And "Eli expostulated with his sons for their wickedness; but they hearkened not for the Lord would slay them[29]." So David conceived it possible enough, that Saul's persecution of him, might be from the Lord, for some sin that he had committed: and so, also, in the Text under consideration, it is said, that "The Lord's anger was kindled against Israel, and therefore he moved David against them to number them -- to draw on them a trespass, with respect to an ordinance which himself had given them. What! did God draw on them a trespass? Was he any ways concerned in making them transgress his own ordinance? We have said so; and doubt not but his providence was concerned. But observe -- that this ordinance (and many others which God gave unto Israel, his people, by Moses) had nothing morally good or evil in it. The reason, why God chose this people to be his people,

---

[26] 2 Chron. xviii. 31.
[27] I Sam, xxvi. 19.
[28] I Kings ii. 15.
[29] I Sam. ii. 25.

was, that he might, through them, manifest himself unto all the world[30]: and one reason, why he gave them so many external ordinances, was, that he might manifest himself the sooner and more clearly: for these external ordinances enabled the surrounding nations to judge, with the greater certainty, of the obedience or disobedience of Israel, unto the Lord their God: and when they also saw a blessing or curse follow (and these too were visible that they might see) what could tend more to extort this confession, "THE LORD, HE IS THE GOD:" for the Gods of the nations never appeared to do good or to do evil -- to execute the least judgment or justice upon earth -- to save or to destroy. Therefore, tho' many of the ordinances, which the Lord gave unto Israel, had naturally no goodness in them: yet it was good for the world that such ordinances were given: it was good not only for those who were near, but even for those who were afar off -- the former would see, and the latter would hear, how the Lord walked with Israel: and the conclusion was near unto both -- that there was no God like unto the Lord -- none, whose works, were like unto his works. When the Mosaic Dispensation, with its ceremonial Law, attended with the temporal blessing and curse, is considered in this light, it will appear, every way worthy of God, -- founded in wisdom, and goodness, and grace. And tho' Israel was a stiff-necked people, that neither did nor could prevent the Lord from manifesting himself, through them: for if they forsook him and his ordinances, so that he could not bless them in the eye of the surrounding nations, then the curse took place: and the Lord set visible marks of his displeasure upon them, and upon the land which he had given them. In the day of transgression, when they refused to hearken and obey, he made the plagues of the people grievous: and their Land, which was as the garden of Eden, became like the country of Sodom and Gomorrha, Admah, and Zeboim, which the Lord overthrew in his anger and in his wrath: so that the next Generation, and their children, and the stranger that came from far, -- even all Nations should see the Lord's

---

[30] See Exodus vii. 5. and Numb. xiv. 21.

doings, and say, "Wherefore hath the Lord done thus unto this land? what meaneth the heat of this great anger?" The answer was near and ready -- "Because they have forsaken the covenant of the Lord, the God of their Fathers[31]." Hence, if he could not teach the Nations, by blessing his people, that he was good and gracious, a rewarder of them who diligently sought him; he taught them, at least, by the curse, that he was a God executing judgment and justice, and truth in respect of his word and promise -- that vengeance belonged unto him and he would repay. There is no doubt, however, but a neglect of moral precepts, and a disobedient heart, were always most displeasing in the eye of God: and the Lord might often see sufficient cause, to correct his people for hypocrisy, for close and secret sins, whilst, in the eye of men, they kept his ordinances. He might justly have smitten, when the surrounding Nations could not well know, wherefore the Lord had done the thing. But he forbare till their transgression became manifest: and his providence might sometimes be concerned in making it so, that his judgments might be manifested also, and teach the world righteousness. Thus the sons of Eli were far gone in wickedness before their father expostulated with them: that God whose priests they were could not be pleased with their doings; nay, he had determined to make his wrath known, and therefore defeated the effect of their Father's counsel, that, by making them ensamples, he might teach future Priests to shun their crimes: and when their wickedness was fully ripe, in the eyes of all the people, he cut them both down, in one day. Thus, also, in the case before us, Israel had displeased the Lord, and his anger was kindled against them, before he moved David, to say, "Go number them." -- They were already vessels of wrath fitted to destruction, however close and secret their wickedness might be: and therefore did he move David to draw on them a trespass, in respect of an external ordinance -- by which visible trespass, and the visible judgment that followed it, the surrounding nations, those of them at least, who had eyes to

---

[31] Deut. xxix. 18. to 29.

see and ears to hear, might surely profit. But be it remembered, that, the Lord did not move David to draw his people into a trespass against any moral law: and recollect also, that the judgment inflicted was temporal only. As to the judgment of the great day, when God shall judge the quick and the dead, we only know, that the judge of all the earth will certainly do right. However it was that David was moved to number the people, he did not perceive it as a notice from God: for his heart smote him when he had done the thing: and indeed as he had an express command not to number them, without the ransom; nothing but an express command to the contrary, would have been a sufficient dispensation: besides, the instruments, whereby God effects his purposes, are not always innocent.

He may move the blood-thirsty to slay the guilty rather than the innocent: but bloodshed is not therefore excusable in the agent: he that thirsteth after blood is a murtherer in principle, and the Lord only directs that principle to his own wise ends, making it subservient to his providence: so some passion might work in David, which was not good in the sight of God, and this he might convert towards numbering the people, rather than suffer it to take a turn no less wicked, and eventually productive of more evil. Numbering the people was an event, which God made use of to his own glory, and the good of mankind: so our Historian, who was a Prophet, perceived this, and that the thing was from the Lord, tho' David himself did not: his convictions, therefore, were just enough, that he had done foolishly. Thus much on this remarkable piece of history as it stands in the second Book of Samuel. But, The compiler of the first Book of Chonicles informs us that, "SATAN stood up against Israel, and provoked David to number Israel." THE LORD, therefore, moved David, to number the people, BY SATAN -- who was the instrument or means in the hand of the Lord. Thus much we certainly know, that the word Satan signifies an adversary of some sort or other. And, When Solomon's strange wives had drawn him into Idolatry, it is said, that, "The Lord stirred up an adversary unto him, Hadad the Edomiteg:" and again, that, "He stirred up another adversary, Rezon the Son of Eliadah[32]." In the Septuagint this occurs in one and the same verse -- which runs thus "And the Lord raised up Satan to Solomon, Hadad the Edomite, and Rezon the Son of Eliadah -- and they were Satan to Israel all the days of Solomon[33]."

Here the word Satan evidently means, an Adversary, or Adversaries, at war with Solomon and his people Israel. And there can be no reasonable ground of doubt, but that the Satan, who provoked David to number the people, was an Adversary of the same sort -- an Adversary whom the Lord had raised up, threatning him, and his people, with war. Such an Adversary, especially if a powerful one, would naturally suggest to David the thought of numbering his people -- that he might know his strength, and what force, he could, on occasion, bring to the field. The sense of the word Satan, in the above quotation from the Septuagint, is clear and evident to every capacity: that sense therefore is authorized by the Septuagint[34]: and as this ancient version of the Scriptures is mostly (if not always) quoted in the New Testament, we need not wish a better authority: it has the seal of our Lord and his Apostles in matters pertaining to doctrine: but if it had not --- if we should set it on a level only with other ancient authors; yet even then its authority must be sufficient when the sense of a word only is to be determined from it: for the Seventy would doubtless make use of words in the same sense in which they themselves, and others of their times, understood them. We have therefore already attained to a clear and determinate sense of the word Satan, under the hand of the Seventy interpreters: and we may be certain, that in their times, it denoted an Adversary or an Enemy at war with Israel: this sense doth easily and naturally dissolve a seeming inconsistency between two parallel Scriptures, which hath been, in these latter times, not

---

[32] I Kings xi. 14--23.
[33] Vide LXX. I Kings xi. 14.
[34] This sense is authorized from other passages in the Hebrew; but as the Author is not skilled in that language, he chooses to rest on the authority of the Septuagint alone.

a little excruciating to interpreters and commentators: since, therefore, by applying a sense clearly ascertained in one passage, the inconsistency between two others hath vanished at once, this stamps a value upon our discovery, and should teach us, not wantonly to depart from that sense of scripture terms, which the scriptures themselves have clearly discovered: for it is easy to see, in the case before us, that we may be greatly misled by Traditions and Systems. We conclude therefore, that as the Lord raised up Satan, or an Adversary, unto Solomon, Hadad the Edomite, and Rezon the Son of Eliadah, and that as they were Satan, or Adversaries, unto Israel, all the days of Solomon; so when the anger of the Lord was kindled against Israel he raised up Satan, an Adversary, i. e. some neighbouring King or Kings, and by this means did he move David against them to say go number Israel: for, when such an Adversary stood up, he provoked David to number his men of war: and in doing this he and his people trespassed against the Lord. When a word has once acquired a meaning, distinct and different from that which was in the writer's mind, and which he intended to convey; it is no wonder if the passages, wherein such word occurs, should be perplexed and difficult: Ideas to which the writer was a perfect stranger, present themselves unto the reader: hence, the connection becomes broken or dismembered, and the sense of the passage incoherent, if not contradictory. Thus the reader, with his own Ideas, strives in vain to understand his author, and thinks the fault is in the book, which is only in his own understanding: This, I am afraid, is often the case with such as complain of great difficulties in scripture: for tho' there should be some things hard to be understood, from the very nature of the subject, yet this will never be complained of by those, who understand the more easy (but not less weighty) matters, contained in the sacred volume. But if, through the ignorance or craft of men in ages past, any considerable number of scripture terms, lost their primitive meanings and acquired new ones, this would spread a vail of darkness over the whole: and it will never be removed till the primitive meanings are ascertained and restored: through the blessing of God upon the labours of his servants, who have sought the truth in the love of it, and in his own word, much hath been done in late times: but there is still work for the skilful scribe: and tho' he has the labours of many good and learned men before him, it is not his business to dwell too much upon them; but rather to search the scriptures, and to contribute his mite to theirs, by adding such observations, as a close attention to the original, may enable him to make: and the less he is held in bondage by preconceived opinions, the more likely he will be to discover the truth: for we shall profit more, if we come to read the scriptures without any Ideas annexed to the terms, than with wrong ones. To exemplify this in the case before us -- If any man had thought himself wholly ignorant of the sense of the word Satan, and had observed it first in the book of Chronicles, if the sense had not discovered itself at sight, he would have examined the connection -- he would have considered what was most likely to provoke David to number Israel: and it is much if he had not suspected that some Enemy threatened his dominions: he would have read a little further, and have observed, that when Joab, the captain of his host, returned the number, he returned such men only as drew the sword[35]: this would have gone a great way towards removing all his doubts, and would have confirmed him in his conjecture: In the last place, he would have observed the message which the Lord sent unto David by the Prophet, "Choose thee -- either three years famine, or three days pestilence, or three months to be destroyed before thy Foes, while the sword

---

[35] I apprehend, all Israel from twenty years old and upwards were men of war, that drew the sword, as occasion might require: The ordinance had respect to these only; and was given partly, at least, to the end they might not be numbered: Israel were not to regard their number, because their battles were the Lord's: and it was nothing with him to save with many or with few: their strength was to walk humbly with their God-- to keep his covenant, his statutes, and ordinances; which done, one of them should chase a thousand: so that they had little more to do than to "sit still and see the salvation of the Lord." But, to those without, the ordinance had another use.

of thine Enemies overtaketh thee." This still tended to confirm his first apprehensions: for it appears from hence that David had foes at this very time, enemies ready to overtake, and fall upon him: 'tis true God could have raised up an Enemy, in a very short time, if there had not been one already in the field; but his usual working has been, to raise up nation against nation, by means which operate slowly, and give leisure to prepare for the battle. Thus a man, not first misled by his own Ideas, would, most probably, discover the true meaning of the word Satan, in this passage, from the connexion, or thread of the history, without any other assistance; but if he opened his Septuagint, and found the authority we have quoted, it would be impossible for him, afterwards, to entertain a doubt. But how wide is the difference when men are under the influence of wrong Ideas! To this, doubtless, it must have been owing, that commentators have overlooked the true sense, and adopted one absolutely irreconcileable, with the parallel passage in the second book of Samuel. I have called the sense above given the true sense, as I do not see, how the shadow of an objection can be raised. It is true there is no particular mention made of the Adversary or Enemy of David: we are not told from whence he arose, nor what became of him afterwards: but this proves nothing against what has been advanced. The History of David's enemies, wars, battles, &c. would have filled a volume much larger than the Bible: such an History as this the sacred writers had no intention to give: their province was to preserve the memory of God's dealings with his people: and in noting down that signal judgment when the people were numbered, it was sufficient just to observe, that Satan, an Adversary or an Enemy, provoked David to do the thing. If we compare this passage in the Chronicles, with that in the book of Samuel, we shall observe, -- that the difference in the relations hath arisen merely, from the different lights, under which the two writers have viewed the matter, and set it forth: Samuel has traced it to the bottom. He says,

"Again the anger of the Lord was kindled against Israel" -- and therefore he moved David to say "Go number them." They had before been troubled with domestic and foreign wars; but their wickedness was not yet corrected: they had sinned again, for the anger of the Lord was kindled afresh: He had determined to make his wrath known, and therefore moved David, by providential measures, to number this people: and when they had trespassed against one of his external ordinances, making their transgression visible in the eye of the surrounding nations, the Lord, then, made bare his arm, and smote them with the pestilence. The wisdom of this proceeding is evident; had the Lord punished them before, for their close and secret sins, the nations around them would not then have known, wherefore the Lord had done this thing: -- they might have been tempted to think that the Lord was not so good and gracious, nor so tender over his people, as they had heard: nay if Israel had departed from the Lord in heart only, and outwardly observed his ordinances (in which case he might justly have smitten them; yet if he had done so) the people in whose sight they dwelt, might have judged hardly of his judgments, as if he slew the righteous as well as the wicked: but when, by his providence, their transgression was made open and visible in the sight of all men, his righteous judgment would then appear, the arm of the Lord would be revealed, and the nations of the world would receive instruction. The author of the account in Chronicles has not traced the matter so deep; but has related it just as it appeared in the eyes of men: He says, Satan, i. e. an Adversary or an Enemy, stood up against Israel, and provoked David (naturally enough) to number the people: and, he says, the Lord was angry with this thing -- for that he was angry before, none but a prophet, or a man of enlightened understanding could know: For this thing, also the people are said to have been smitten with the pestilence: and so the world would judge; but in strict truth the cause of the judgment laid further back: for the Lord was angry before. From the account in Samuel, compared with that in the Chronicles, we learn -- that the anger of the Lord was kindled against Israel for prior sins, and therefore he[36] raised up Satan, i. e. an Adversary or Enemy, who provoked David to number Israel and Judah -- even all his valiant men that drew the sword: and when they, had thus manifested their transgression, by trespassing an ordinance, which trespass was expressly threatened with a plague, the Lord then smote them with the pestilence; and there died of the plague seventy thousand men. The sense of the word Satan, I Chron. xxi. I. the history contained in the chapter, and the divine proceedings with respect to his people, are, I hope, sufficiently cleared: and tho' I have introduced matters somewhat foreign to my inquiry, yet it is hoped, every attempt to elucidate the scriptures, will be candidly received: add to this, that a little variety, provided it has the least distant relation to the subject, may well be dispensed with, till the subject shall open and enlarge itself. Any further remarks upon the above passage would be impertinent: for as it is incontestibly clear from the Septuagint, i. e. in I Kings xi. 14. that the word Satan doth there signify an Adversary or an Enemy at war with Israel; so when the same sense is applied here, I Chron. xxi. I. it is no less clear that it is the true one: these two passages agree, in supporting one and the same meaning of the word, and authorize us to say, that we have acquired some knowledge of our subject. The authority of the Septuagint is as good an authority as can be wished for, and indeed it is much to be doubted whether we have a better: however, those who understand the Oriental languages need not rest here -- if it may be of any service, in the present case, to seek elsewhere: but as the word Satan is not Greek, it was doubtless retained from the original, which the seventy had before them. The Greek word $\diablos$ has, in scripture, the same sense or signification as the word Satan. This is evident from Esther vii. 4, and viii. I. for Haman, who is called $\dot{o}\ \diablos$, was an

---

[36] 2 Sam. xxiv. I.--This "He" has been tortured to confess what it never meant. It has been said that "It was not the Lord but He, that is, Satan, who moved David." This is straining to reconcile passages it is true; but it will ever remain evident that the word He doth here relate to the Lord, and to nothing else.

Adversary or an Enemy unto Israel: the above passages are rightly translated in our bible -- "The Enemy (or Adversary) could not countervail the King's damage;" and "Ahasuerus gave the house of Haman the jews Enemy unto Esther the Queen[37]." So if we follow the Septuagint version of I Chron. xxi. I, we shall rightly translate "An Enemy stood up against Israel, and provoked David to number Israel[38]." This is good intelligible English, and such as a common soldier would readily understand. THE word Satan next occurs in the 1st and 2nd chapters of Job: where, if a different sense, from that already attained, should seem necessary, it will then be fit to examine the context with the greater care and attention. The learned are not agreed, whether this book ought to be understood as a real History, or as an instructive composition of art. I take it the first opinion is better grounded, and rather to be followed; but it may be necessary to make this concession, that in some parts the author has had recourse to figurative representation. The book begins with the character of Job, who is the principal subject of the History. This character is given in a few plain comprehensive words, comprized within the compass of five verses; but what follows, verse 6th to the 13th -- is not quite so easy to comprehend. It is probable, however, that the difficulty arises from our own Ideas -- from some mistaken notions -- or from want of skill in the Eastern manner of representation: what is written for instruction, as this book doubtless was, should not be clothed with too much mystery, for that would defeat the end proposed: we must conclude, therefore, that the writer was perfectly intelligible to the people of his own times; and that there is a key, if we can but find it, which will easily unlock the mysteries of this book, and open our way to the instruction

---

[37] See the Septuagint. Esther vii. 4. Ὀυ γὰ ἄξιος ὁ διάβολος τῆς αὐλῆς τῦ βασιλέως and viii. I. ὅσα ὑπῆρχεν Ἀμὰν τῷ διαβόλῳ.

[38] I Chron. xxi. I. Καὶ ἔςη διάβολος ἐν τῷ Ἰσραὴλ, ἢ ἐπέσειςε τὸν Δαυὶδ τῦ ἀριθμῆσαι τὸν Ἰσραὴλ.

contained therein. Having given us the character of Job, our authors words are these "Now there was a day when the Sons of God, came to present themselves before the Lord, and Satan came also among them: and the Lord said unto Satan whence comest thou? Then Satan answered the Lord and said, From going to and fro in the earth, and from walking up and down in it. And the Lord said unto Satan, Hast thou considered my servant Job, that there is none like him in the earth, a perfect and an upright man, one that feareth God and escheweth evil? Then Satan answered the Lord and said, Doth Job fear God for nought? Haft not thou made an hedge about him, and about his house, and about all that he hath on every side? Thou haft blessed the work of his hands, and his substance is encreased in the land. But put forth thine hand now and touch all that he hath, and he will curse thee to thy face: And the Lord said unto Satan, Behold all that he hath is in thy power, only upon himself put not forth thine hand. So Satan went forth from the presence of the Lord." Now, Supposing there had been no mistake concerning Satan, but that he were a Being inflexibly wicked, and lost to every spark of goodness -- that his enmity against God neither did nor could abate, and that his malice, unprovoked, were uniformly set to spread corruption and destruction through the works of God--suppose this, and it appears highly incongruous, that such a Being should come into the more immediate presence of God, as Satan is here said to do: and, again, it seems no less incongruous, that God, who is of purer eyes than to behold iniquity, and in whose sight the heavens are not pure, should condescend to speak familiarly with a Being whose impurity and iniquity are supposed to be inconceivably great, and also immutable; yet the Lord is represented as speaking familiarly with Satan -- even as a man doth with his friend; he shews no marks of displeasure against him; but delivers those blessings and comforts of life into his hand, which had before been the portion of his own most righteous servant -- and this only to convince him that his servant was sincere, and served with a voluntary and free service. We may observe further that these words "Hast thou considered my servant Job," are spoken by way of admonition. Satan, or the Adversary, is asked, if he had considered -- if he had duly revolved in his mind[39], the character and virtues of Job, that eminent and faithful servant of the Lord. But this could answer no end, if the words are addressed to a Being lost beyond the reach of mercy, and concluded in a state from whence there is no redemption.

Many other objections might be brought against the received sense of the word Satan, in this passage; but these are sufficient to excite suspicion and attention. Let us therefore look narrowly to the Character, and try if we can fix it with greater certainty -- or so, as may be less liable to exception. We have already seen that the Adversaries or Enemies of Israel, or of the Lord's people, are Satan: such were Hadad the Edomite, and Rezon the Son of Eliadah of Zobah, in the days of Solomon: and as this is the only sense of the word, which we have, as yet, been able to ascertain, it will be proper to try how far it will go, in the present case. When Job, the servant of the one true God, was in his prosperity--when the Most High had blessed him with health and abundance of all things--even in that day "Did the Sons of God come to present themselves before the Lord, and Satan, or the Adversary, came also among them." Now if the Sons of God are Men, it is most natural to suppose that the Adversary is to be understood of Men also -- who were not Sons of God; but Adversaries[40] unto them. But in the Septuagint version of the Scriptures, we do not read the Sons, but the Angels, or Messengers of God: and in order to make the opposition more exact, Satan, the Adversary, may be understood of Angels or Spirits, who in this case opposed themselves. Suppose them such who stood in the presence of God[41]. But observe, The author does not fay that this was any

---

[39] Πρόσεχες τῇ διανοίᾳ σου.

[40] Adversaries of the people of God, were mostly the servants of other Gods -- of Gods that were no Gods. Idolaters.

[41] There is, however, no necessity to suppose them either fallen or evil Angels; but only Angels opposing Angels: and that not really, but in supposition only, for the sake of representation. I see no grounds in scripture to believe that any Angels ever did fall. And that doctrine, as

way revealed to him, either by word, or by vision, or otherwise[42]. We have therefore no authority to understand it in any other light than as a machinery of his own raising, to answer the purpose of representation: And it is so well constructed that it lets us at once, into the reason and use of Job's afflictions. The Sons of God, or his Angels, or Messengers, represent the worshippers of the one true God, and Satan is the representative of their Adversaries: The parties are brought into the presence of God to instruct us that his providence directed, and why, and what, he did direct. Satan or the Adversary, is asked whence he came -- but surely this question, which our author has put into the mouth of the Lord, was put altogether for our sakes: known unto God are all his works, and there is no creature which is not manifest in his sight; but to prevent mistakes it might be necessary that we should be informed that Satan, or the Adversary, goeth to and fro in the earth, and walketh up and down in it. Here we shall be sure to find the Adversaries of the Lord's people; but Job's Adversaries are here more particularly marked, who were rovers and wanderers

---

now received, is liable to great exceptions. Supposing an Arcangel, and a whole order of angelic Beings, to have unhappily sinned against God their common Father; yet who shall say that He, "whose tender mercies are over all his works," would have shewn no mercy to such Sons? -- or that "judgment without mercy" begun at the head of the creation, when not a sparrow falls to the ground without our Heavenly Father? Besides, it is not easy to be conceived, how so many of the perfectest of created Beings should degenerate, at once, into mere abstracts of malice and wickedness.

[42] We may observe that the book of Job is wrote throughout in the Historical Stile: and when the author says, that "There was a day when the Sons, Angels, or Messengers of God, came to present themselves before the Lord, and Satan came also among them" -- he gives not the least intimation that he was a prophet; but this he should have done, if he had hoped to be understood literally as speaking of facts which no human eye could see, and which could not be known, but by immediate revelation. It is therefore most reasonable to conclude that the representation is figurative.

that lived by plunder and depredations[43]. This Satan, or the Adversary, had an opportunity of observing and profiting by the example of Job, a most eminent servant of the true God: and therefore another question is put with great propriety, "Hast thou confidered my servant Job, that there is none like him (my servant) in the earth, a perfect and upright man, one that feareth God and escheweth evil." God is glorified in his Saints that are upon earth: and he appeals to their adversaries, themselves being judges, whether the excellency of his service is not manifest in the excellency of his servants. His servant Job was the best, and he had made him the greatest also, of all the men in the East, that the Adversary might see, and consider, and know, that the blessing of the Lord is upon them that fear him. The Lord therefore asks that question which his providence asked daily, "hast thou considered my servant Job?" The Adversary had confidered, or at least had observed, both his piety and his greatness; yet conversion did not follow: the answer was ready -- "Doth Job fear God for nought? hast not thou made an hedge about him, and about his house, and about all that he hath on every side? thou has blessed the work of his hands, and his substance is encreased in the land. But put forth thine hand now and touch all that he hath, and he will curse thee to thy face." Satan is here made to deliver his own sentiments; and nothing can be more characteristic: it has always been the Lot of the Lord's servants to be evil spoken of, to be charged with hypocrisy and worldly views. The Adversary, or Adversaries, have never done them justice in this respect. The worshippers of strange Gods, did not deny the Lord to be a God -- nor yet that he protected and blessed his servants[44]: the arm of the Lord was too often, and too clearly, revealed to leave them in doubt of the above matters; but still they looked unto their own Gods, and would not

---

[43] The Sabeans and Chaldeans; οἱ αἰχμαλωτίοντες ᾗ οἱ ἱπσεῖς; yet the word Satan need not be understood of them only: but rather as having a distant respect to all the adverfaries of the people of God.
[44] Kings xx. 23. -- 28.

acknowledge that his servants were more excellent than their neighbours. Thus the Adversary said, Job is bribed to his service; doth he serve for nought -- with a free and voluntary service? no: he, his house, and all that he hath, is hedged about on every side: but let the Lord his God bring him into troubles like other men -- let the Lord put the cup of affliction into his hand, and see whether he will not change his God, or curse the Lord even to his face. A better defence could not be put into the mouth of the Adversary: there is weight in every part of it: for if Job's service was not free, wherein was it to be accounted of? Blessed, all around, an hypocrite might serve: and perhaps nothing, but a reverse of fortune, could effectually convince the Adversary, that their estimate was false. The Lord says of his people who obey his voice, ye are my peculiar treasure; but all the earth is mine: even the Adversaries of his people are his -- the work of his hands: and tho' they have erred from his ways, his providence is concerned to bring them back unto himself. His servants are his priests through whom he makes himself known: His praise is in their fidelity, and he crowns it with glory and honour. So here Job is called forth to suffer for his sake; that the Adversary might see and know, that it is the Lord that maketh poor and maketh rich; that bringeth low and lifteth up -- and that his servants are the excellent upon earth. Therefore, that Job might glorify the Lord in adversity as well as in prosperity -- the Lord said unto Satan, or the Adversary, "Behold all that he hath is in thy power -- only upon himself put not forth thine hand." Hereby the author of this book has given us to understand, that Job was delivered unto affliction, of the Lord -- for the conviction and instruction of the Adversary. Thus far all is clear: let us now see how far this sense is confirmed or combated by the sequel. When all that Job had, even all his substance, was delivered into the hand of Satan or of the Adversary, observe what became of them. Whilst his oxen were plowing in the field, and the asses feeding beside them -- the Sabeans fell upon them and took them away, and slew the servants with the sword: The fire of God fell from heaven, and burnt up the sheep, and the servants, and consumed them: The

Chaldeans made out three bands, and fell upon the camels and carried them away, and slew the servants with the sword: and whilst his sons and his daughters were eating and drinking in their eldest brother's house -- behold, there came a great wind from the wilderness, and smote the four corners of the house, and it fell upon them and they died. Thus was Job stript of all that he had: and we see by whose power, or by whose hand. The Enemy is not hid. -- His Adversaries the Sabeans and Chaldeans have possessed themselves, at least, of his oxen, his asses, and his camels: and have slain his servants, who kept them, with the edge of the sword: they have contributed most largely to pluck him bare: and therefore it is reasonable to conclude, that Satan, or the Adversary, is to be understood chiefly of them: and it was because of them, or for their sake, that the fire of God fell upon his sheep and shepherds -- and that a great wind from the wilderness smote the house of his eldest son, and buried all his children in the ruins: -- but if this is not satisfactory, recollect "that the very stars from heaven, once fought against Sisera:" and here the elements themselves become Satan, or Adversaries, unto Job. Lightning has deprived him of his sheep and shepherds, and a great wind of his sons and, daughters. We have now seen the power or powers that prevailed against Job: and if you would know in whose hand they originally are, take the information from his own mouth. These are his words. "The Lord gave, and the Lord hath taken away, blessed be the name of the Lord." So then, "In all this Job sinned not, neither did he charge the Lord his God foolishly;" but the Adversary was not yet put to silence: and therefore Job is again called forth, to suffer yet more for their sake. Hence, our author erects his scenery a second time. "Again (says he) there was a day, when the Sons (Angels or Messengers) of God, came to present themselves before the Lord, and Satan (or the Adversary) came also among them to present himself before the Lord. And the Lord said unto Satan from whence comest thou? and Satan answered the Lord, and said, from going to and fro in the earth, and from walking up and down in it. And the Lord said unto Satan, Hast thou considered my servant Job, that there is none like him in the earth, a perfect and an upright man, one that feareth God, and escheweth evil? And still he holdeth fast his integrity, although thou movedst me against him, to destroy (or rather to afflict) him without a cause." These last words, ought not, by any means, to be understood as if they were spoken to a real evil, or wicked spirit, incapable of repentance or amendment: for if such a Being did ever exist, he could not possibly move the Lord to destroy, or even to afflict, his righteous servants, without a cause: should this be admitted it will clearly overthrow the most certain knowledge we have of God, either from reason or revelation. But if by Satan we are to understand the Adversaries or Enemies of the Lord's people, or if they are included in the Idea, then for their sakes, that they may be converted and saved, the Lord may afflict the most righteous of his servants, and that too, when there is no cause in themselves: and it is a known truth, that the first christians were afflicted, and many of them delivered up unto cruel deaths, not for their own sakes, but for the unbelieving world -- for the sake of their Adversaries, who were ready enough to believe them hypocrites in the day of prosperity: however when they were permitted to try their fidelity, and found them hold fast their integrity in the midst of affliction -- when they saw and considered the firm unshaken faith and virtue of the servants of Christ -- even the Adversary himself (in many of his members) glorified God by believing on him. And such, or a like reason, we are taught to assign, for the sufferings of Job. As in the former case, so in this, the parties are brought into the presence of God, to inform us that providence directed in all that befel this eminent man: and the dialogue marks out beyond a possibility of mistake (provided only the terms are understood) the reason and end of his sufferings. Satan, or the Adversary, is asked if he had considered Job, the servant of the Lord, -- that still, in all his affliction, he held fast his integrity. This should have wrought conviction; but it seems there was still an evasion: for Satan answered the Lord and said -- "Skin for skin, (or skin after skin) yea all that a man hath will he give for his life. But put forth thine hand now, and touch his bone and his flesh, and he will curse thee to thy face." The sentiment conveyed in these words is -- that the prospect of death brought near, would shake the integrity, or manifest the hypocrisy, of Job: so did the Adversary judge of the disciples of Christ, and they too were permitted to try the experiment. So, now, That the mouth of the Adversary might be stopped -- that they might see, and consider, and be convinced. "The Lord said unto Satan, (the Adversary) Behold he is in thine hand, but save his life[45]. So Satan went forth from the presence of the Lord, and smote Job with sore boils, from the sole of his foot unto his crown." It is sufficient to justify the expression that Satan smote him, if he was smitten on Satan's account, or for his cause. Thus if an innocent man is brought to the block, we overlook the judge and executioner, and charge the false witnesses with the innocent blood. So the blood of Christ is sometimes charged upon the rulers of the Jews, and sometimes on the whole house of Israel, tho' both the sentence of death, and the execution of it, proceeded from other people. They who were so active in procuring his death, crucified the Lord of life: and the judge and executioners, are mostly, if not always, overlooked. We might perhaps have found instances still nearer the case of Job; but the above is near enough to shew, that the stroke is not always imputed to the hand that strikes it. And tho' Satan is here said to have smitten Job with sore boils, yet if Job himself was not mistaken he received this evil at the hand of God. So also did his wife and friends, and all who saw him, determine. It is the determination of reason and common sense, which we may safely abide by: and this author has, here only, imputed it to Satan, or the Adversary, to the end that we might know, for whose sake or on whose account he was smitten. It may be fit, however, to keep in view the machinery of this author: He makes Job's Adversaries appear in the presence of God by a representative, bearing their name and character: and whatsoever was done by them, or for their sakes, this representative is said to do: for them the elements

---

[45] Observe, that this grant, as well as a former, is given to convince Satan of his mistake: Cui bono? if such a Being as is usually apprehended?

became Adversaries to Job--fire fell from heaven and burnt up his sheep and his shepherds, and a wind from the wilderness deprived him of his children--for them also he was smitten of sore boils: now it was fit that all this should once, at least, be charged to the Adversaries account; for without this we should not have known that they were concerned in it: but how shall it be charged on their representative? why, commit the elements into his hands, and let him have power to smite with boils -- let him use this power, and the thing is done. There is the greater propriety in this representation of the Adversary; because the lightning and wind, and second cause of the boils, did really stand over against Job, and became Satan or Adversaries unto him -- joining issue with his other Adversaries: and the representative would not have been complete, without they were represented also: So that the Idea of Satan may, if necessary, be extended as far as there is an Adversary to be taken in: we may add also, that it was no unusual thing among the ancients, to give an animate representative to things inanimatev, and to second causes[46] of which they were entirely ignorant: instances of this abound in scripture, and the best of the heathen poets have immortalized their names by the excellency of their representations in this way. The commandment was delivered unto the Lord's people of old in these words -- "Hear, O ISRAEL, the Lord our God is one Lord. And THOU shalt love the Lord THY God, with all THINE heart." Nobody entertains a doubt but that this is addressed to the people at large. It certainly was.--But how is it addressed to them?--plainly in the person of Israel their Father, who is here, and elsewhere, THEIR REPRESENTATIVE: to HIM the commandment is delivered: and yet the people always understood that it was delivered unto THEM. They never once thought of setting aside the commandment, because it was delivered to their representative only. They well knew that such a distinction would have been

---

[46] Numb. xvi. 30. "If the earth open her mouth and swallow, &c." Jeremiah xlvi. 10. "The sword shall devour, shall be satiated, and made drunk with their blood." Isaiah iv. 4. "The spirit of burning." Luke xiii. 11. "A spirit of infirmity."

foolish and vain. and it is no less so to distinguish between Satan and the Adversaries of the Lord's people: for Satan is as much a representative of the one, as Israel is of the other. Again, the language, and acts of Israel, are, in this case, understood to be the language and acts of a people: and as Satan is equally a representative, his language and acts ought to be interpreted by the same rule: we have applied them to a people in the case before us, (i. e. in the case of Job) and the reader may judge with what propriety. We may further observe that the words Israel and Satan, when applied in this sense, are both APPELLATIVES, and consequently ought not to be understood of an individual, but of many: thus David numbered Israel -- and Hadad, Rezon, and their forces, were Satan to Israel -- as the Sabeans and Chaldeans were unto Job. And thus THE ADVERSARY, in our own language, which answers to Satan, or ὁ διάβολος, is frequently applied to any unfriendly nation. And tho' this remark is anticipated just above, and in the foregoing pages, it may not be improper to recommend it to the reader's particular notice, as it confirms, and is confirmed by, the sense of an able critic on the oriental languages[47], who has endeavoured to prove that the Hebrew article prefixed to the word Satan, in this book of Job, makes it an appellative. But, after all, it must be allowed that the representation, in this case, is carried somewhat higher than in common cases; and the reasons for it are obvious: for Satan, or the Adversary, was here to be brought into the presence of the Lord, and to speak with him face to face, that we might, hereby, know why and wherefore Job was afflicted of the Lord: and as it was necessary for the conviction of Satan, or the Adversary, that Job should be visited by affliction from different quarters, that the elements should conspire with them to strip him of his substance, and deprive him of his children, as also that he himself should be smitten with sore boils; so this power was to be committed unto their representative: otherwise we should not have known that all this was -- because of the Adversary: and,

---

[47] MICHAELIS -- in his Remarks on Dr Lowth's Prelections.

moreover, there would have been an evident defect in the representation, if any thing or cause (apparent or hid) which contributed to Job's fall or affliction, had been excluded from the Idea of the Adversary: for the Adversary cannot properly be said to do more than the Adversaries represented hereby are able to effect: hence the Idea to be annexed to Satan, in this place, must include all those adverse powers which contributed to the fall, and deep distress, of this Hero in affliction. But to form an Idea of the representative independent, or abstracted from, the represented, is of little consequence: the Adversaries might have been represented by a body of angels or spirits assuming their character: and if we add one who can cast forth lightnings -- another to unbridle the winds -- a third to smite with boils, there will need no more. Such a group, however, would seem to want a representative, in order to address them as one: and it is much more natural to suppose that the author has personified all Job's Adversaries in one -- who bears upon him the whole of their character -- speaks their language -- and does their works: and that this person might be complete, wanting nothing, he commits the elements, and a power of smiting with boils, into his hands. And thus he becomes a perfect representative of all Job's Adversaries, of what sort or nature soever. This Being, who is all over of the writer's creation, he names -- Satan: The Adversary. This name is appellative, which shews us that it is not to be understood of one, but of many -- he confesses himself a sojourner on earth -- exposes his character with his own mouth -- goes forth, and does that, which the author himself, without a figure, declares to have been done by the Adversaries -- or else by the finger of God. So that if the writer is now misunderstood, it must be a difficult matter to guard against misapprehension: for the name, or appellation of Satan being, in scripture, plainly applied to the Adversaries or Enemies of the Lord's people, that alone should have been sufficient to prevent any gross mistakes -- especially as the sense naturally passes to other adverse powers, that may occasionally arise: and in the present case we are expressly told by what persons and means Job was stript of his substance and afflicted: consequently we have nothing more to do, than to extend the Idea of the Adversary to such persons and means. Upon the whole of the matter, we come to this conclusion, viz. that the author of the book of Job, has had recourse to personification, that he might, by that means, bring Job's Adversaries into the presence of God, and by a short dialogue inform us, at once, of the reason and end of that man's sufferings. This personification is judiciously managed: there is both elegance and propriety in including such adverse powers of nature as became Satan unto Job. It contracts the History -- is perfectly agreeable to the Eastern manner of writing, and might be exemplified by many instances drawn from the Greek and Latin poets -- whose chief excellence consists in this sort of representation[48]. The passages we have been considering, when understood in this light, become a key to the whole book, which would be instructive both to the Jew and to the Gentile: the former, being the people of God, might learn from it to endure all things for the Lord's sake -- that the Adversary might be convinced of the integrity of his servants, and of his power to destroy or to save; which power is manifested in the deep affliction and subsequent exaltation of his servant Job: and the latter, the Gentile, or the Adversaries themselves, might learn that there was no God like unto the Lord, who bringeth low and raiseth up -- who supports his servants under affliction, and faileth not to turn the captivity of them who put their trust in him: and they might learn also, that the Lord in mercy and grace to them afflicted his righteous servants, that they might see and hear and be converted unto him. Instruction, in this view, rises from every part of the History; and so obviously that it will not be necessary to proceed further in pointing it out. The sense in which the word Satan is now understood has drawn a veil over the whole, by introducing an Idea foreign to the matter: and the two passages, wherein the word occurs, instead of serving as a key,

---

[48] We need but read a few pages in the first book of Virgil's Æneiad to be convinced. The council of the Gods, Book X, is grounded on the same plan of representation with this in Job.

have been rendered exceedingly difficult, if not absolutely unintelligible, by the intervention of this wrong Idea. And this alone is a sufficient reason for rejecting it. But if the received opinion relative to Satan, is not well founded in scripture, and if a different sense hath been clearly made out, it will then follow, that the received notion should be rejected, till we find some good reasons in justification of it. And these, I am pretty certain, will not be found in this book of Job. The personification alone has solved all difficulties: and the writer himself teaches us to consider it in no other light, when, in the subsequent parts of the History, we are expressly told, that the Lord brought all this evil upon Job -- He himself considers his boils as proceeding from the immediate hand of God: his wife was doubtless, of the same persuasion, when she said "Dost thou still retain thine integrity? curse God and die." -- His friends argue upon the supposition that God afflicted him for his sins -- Elihu the son of Barachel, who speaks as an oracle of God, supposes him to be chastised of the Lord, that he might be made more perfect through sufferings -- The Lord himself (Chap. xl. 8.) is introduced, by the author, acknowledging the matter as his judgment -- and lastly all Job's brethren and sisters, and all that had been of his acquaintance, came unto him, and bemoaned and comforted him, over all the evil that the Lord had brought upon him. To all this we may yet add, that Elihu, who speaks for the Lord, or the Lord himself, doth, in this very book, claim the direction of the lightning and winds, by which Job suffered so much, and they are said expressly to be immediately subject to, or under the immediate direction of, the Lord: it is asserted also, that he layeth trouble and affliction upon the loins of men, and chasteneth them: the Lord therefore smote Job with sore boils -- and when it is said that Satan smote him, we cannot allow any more than the personification of a second cause immediately in the hand of God, which became Satan or an Adversary to Job, just as lightning and wind were in the same hand Adversaries unto him in a former case: for to suppose a real separate spirit, studiously set to counteract the will of God, had any concern in these matters, would be taking the reins of government out of the hand of God, and committing them to one who would be sure to make the most perverse use of them -- and it could never be said that his works were the Lord's doings. Such a notion clogs the history with innumerable difficulties: we are therefore justified in taking up a more obvious sense, which removes all difficulties, and substitutes sound wisdom and instruction in their place. Here I shall leave the reader to make what further reflections he pleases, -- knowing no objections that will lay against the interpretation adopted in the foregoing pages, but such as might be made to the most admired passages in the writings of the best ancient authors -- and to poetic representation in general. We shall now proceed to, Psalm cix. 6. where we read "Set thou a wicked man over him, and let Satan stand at his right hand." Or as it is elsewhere translated "Set thou an ungodly man to be ruler over him, and let Satan stand at his right hand." It is not clear to me what prevented the translators of our Bible from interpreting the word Satan in this passage: they certainly knew that it signified an Adversary; and if it had been so translated no body would have been at a loss to understand it: for as the devoted person, has a wicked man given him for his ruler, it will be universally allowed, that another may do for his Adversary -- especially when set so near as "at his right hand" -- ready to resist and molest him on all occasions. In the Septuagint version, the word Satan is translated $\delta\iota\alpha\beta o\lambda o\varsigma$ -- without the article: this points out the most limited and restrained (or, at least, the most simple) sense of the word: in English, an Adversary. The passage is too clear to need enlarging upon: I shall therefore only observe further -- that Adversaries in matters of legal strife, are said to have stood, formerly, at the right hand of the person accused by them; and if so, the phrase "Let Satan, or an Adversary, stand at his right hand," may be supposed to point out such an Adversary. This will make some alteration in the case of the devoted person: for as a wicked man was to be his ruler, or judge, his circumstances became more desperate, when an Adversary stood at his right hand and accused him.

ONCE more only in our English Bible, doth the word Satan occur. This is in the prophecy of Zechariah, Chap. iii. I. 2. We may observe here, that from the I st to the 6th Chapter, inclusive, is one continued prophecy, relative to the restoration of the Jews, and the rebuilding of the Temple (after the Babylonian captivity) under the conduct of Zerubbabel, the chief ruler of the Jews, and of Joshua the High Priest. The passage to be considered is a part of the prophecy, and runs in the following words. "And he (i. e. the Lord) shewed me Joshua the high priest standing before the Angel of the Lord, and Satan standing at his right hand to resist (or to oppose) him. And the Lord said unto Satan, The Lord rebuke thee, O Satan, even the Lord that hath chosen Jerusalem rebuke thee." This is evidently and professedly a prophetic vision -- intended, as all such visions were, to figure out something future to be fulfilled in the world. Joshua (or Jesus, as it is in the Greek) the then high priest, appears in the vision, and was one of the parties: Satan, or the Adversary, resisted or opposed him, and consequently was another party: but the Lord stood with Joshua, and rebuked the Adversary. However, neither Joshua nor Satan were here, but only their visionary representatives -- called by the names of the persons they were intended to represent. The vision presents us with scenery only -- a mere picturesque representation, which vanished and disappeared before the real actors stood up, and entered upon their respective parts. We suppose then, that Joshua, sometime or other, had really to do with an Adversary, or Adversaries; -- that the Lord stood with him, and rebuked the opposer. If we turn to the book of Ezra, which contains a short history of these times, I shall find the vision explained by facts. Chap. v. begins thus, "Then the prophets, Haggai the prophet, and Zechariah the son of Iddo, prophesied unto the Jews that were in Judah and Jerusalem, in the name of the God of Israel -- then rose up Zerubbabel the son of Shealtiel, and Joshua the son of Jozadak, and began to build the house of God which is at Jerusalem, and with them were the prophets of God helping them." -- strengthening their hands, at least, with the word of prophecy. There is no doubt then, but that the prophecy of

Zechariah was delivered about this time: Chap. iii. is addressed to Joshua, and Chap. iv. to Zerubbabel, to encourage them in their undertaking; i. e. in rebuilding the Temple. Joshua, however, is forewarned (in the vision) of an Adversary whom the Lord would rebuke -- as was Zerubbabel also in the next chapter. So Ezra proceeds, and informs us -- that "At the same time (i. e. whilst they were building) came unto them Tatnai, Governour on this side the river, and Shethar-boznai, and their companions, and said thus unto them, Who hath commanded you to build this house, and to make up this wall? -- And what are the names of the men that make this building?" In short, they would have made them cease from building, and wrote to Darius for that purpose; but it stands recorded that "The Eye of God was upon the Elders of the Jews (upon Joshua more especially, who was high priest over the House of God) so that the Adversary or Adversaries could not cause them to cease till the matter came before Darius," -- who made a decree, that they should not only suffer the building to go on, but assist the builders with such things as might be needful. Thus was the prophecy of Zechariah fulfilled. The Lord stood with Joshua, and rebuked the Adversary. The Lord stood, indeed, with his people at large; but as Joshua was at the head of them, in so exalted a station, more particularly in respect of the temple, so it may properly be said, that the Lord stood with Joshua, under whose conduct the work was carrying on. Not that we are to except Zerubbabel who was prince of the Children of Israel: the Adversaries resisted him, as well as Joshua: and the Lord declared, by the mouth of the same prophet, that his hands had laid the foundation of the house, and that his hands should also finish it -- notwithstanding any Adversaries who might oppose him; but as the word of the Lord is directed, separately, to the two chiefs of of the house of Israel; so Joshua alone is concerned, in that part of the prophecy, which I am now concerned to explain. That Satan ought, here, to be understood of Tatnai, who is called Governor on this side the river, of Shethar-boznai, and his companions (Deputy Governors I suppose who acted in conjunction with them) will not admit of any reasonable doubt.

'Tis true any one of them might have been called Satan, when he became an Adversary; but ὁ Σατᾶν, with the article, or διάβολος as in the Septuagint, must either be understood of some eminent Adversary, or else collectively of the Adversaries: and it is very clear that the seventy have understood the word of more than one: for we read only of Joshua and Satan, standing before the Angel of the Lord; and yet the Angel commanded those who stood before him, to take away Joshua's filthy garments -- and let them, said he, set a fair mitre upon his head, and they did so. This is doubtless to be understood of Satan or the Adversary, and was fulfilled, when Darius sent his decree to these Governors, that they should assist the Jews, out of the King's goods, by allowing them expences out of the tribute beyond the river, and by supplying them with such things as they had need of: which decree the Adversaries [49] were obliged to comply with, at their peril. See the decree, Ezra Chap. vi. I shall only further observe, that prophetic visions are more or less striking, in the resemblance they have to things signified by them, as it hath seemed good to the Divine Wisdom, to convey a clear or obscure notice of things future. This vision was for the immediate encouragement of Joshua, and the figures appearing, are the figures of the very persons, who would be actors in the business, of which the prophet spoke: it was indeed too clear to be mistaken -- unless you suppose Satan a mere spirit[50]: that indeed will cover the passage with darkness and mystery. We have now gone through the Old

---

[49] I It seems that they were seven in number, and that they are the seven eyes mentioned Zech. iii. 9. and iv. 10. also, that Darius was the stone laid before Joshua, the golden candlestick, and one of the anointed ones who stood up for the Lord of the whole earth. The seven lamps of the candlestick, the seven Princes or Privy Councellors of Darius, and the seven pipes to the seven lamps, the seven deputy Governors, who, tho' once Adversaries, afterwards assisted the Jews according to the word of the Lord.

[50] If a separate spirit only had been rebuked, the Adversaries might still have impeded the building of the Temple.

Page 118

Testament: the word Satan occurs no more in the English Bible: and I have, occasionally, taken notice where, and in what sense, it occurs in the Septuagint; here it is always translated by διάβολος, or ὁ διάβολος, except I Kings, xi. 14. How oft it is found in the Hebrew, must be left to the examination of those, who are conversant in that language. It only remains that we should collect the information we have gained, and that we should take it along with us to the New Testament. We have seen that the word Satan (or its correspondent Greek term διάβολος) is applied to such persons as were adversaries or enemies of the people of God. Thus Hadad the Edomite, and Rezon the son of Eliadah were Satan unto Israel all the days of Solomon[51] -- and Satan (an Adversary whose name is not mentioned) stood up against Israel, and provoked David to number his men of war[52]. In both these cases Satan is to be understood of an Adversary or Enemy at war with Israel. In the time of the captivity, Haman, the son of Hammedatha, the Agaggite, was -- ὁ διάβολος, the Adversary of the Jews. This man, under Ahasuerus King of Persia and Media, projected a violent persecution, and thought to have destroyed all the children of the captivity[53]. Here the Adversary is a Persecutor of the people of God, and one who accused them unto the King under whom they were captive: so in the book of Psalms, where it is written, "Set thou a wicked man to be ruler over him, and let Satan stand at his right hand[54]." --Satan, the Adversary, is either a Persecutor, or, which is more probable, an accuser -- for the right hand of the accused was the place of the accuser. Thus far we may venture to say all is clear. Zechariah had a vision in which the Lord shewed him Joshua the high priest, and Satan standing at his right hand. This Adversary was a persecutor, or rather, for the reason above given, an accuser. It may I think be

---

[51] See I Kings, xi. 14. Septuagintver.
[52] I Chron. xxi. i. &c.
[53] Book of Esther, Chap. iii. also vii. and viii.
[54] Psalm cix. 6.

admitted that a prophetic vision is, as much as any other, "A baseless fabric, which vanishes -- and leaves not a wreck behind." But the interpretation is sure: and this prophetic vision was fulfilled -- when Tatnai, Shethar-boznai, and his companions resifted Joshua in building the Temple, and sent an accusation against him and his people to Darius the King[55]. These deputy Governors were really Satan to Joshua and his people Israel: so that this vision is perfectly cleared by facts. The author of the book of Job has had recourse to poetic representation, which has in it something of the visionary cast, but is well adapted to the purpose of instruction: a few examples of this kind are found in scripture, where the poetic licence is taken in its full extent[56]: and how frequently this is done by the best heathen writers, nobody who has read will need to be informed. In the above-named book, the author has personified all Job's adversaries in one -- who is their representative. By this means he has brought Satan into the immediate presence of God, and made way for the introduction of a short dialogue, by which we are informed that God delivered up his servant to affliction, for the conviction and conversion of the Adversaries, or of Satan. The Adversary, in this case, was the Sabeans and Chaldeans, for whose sake the lightenings and winds became Adversaries to Job, and he was also smitten with sore boils. The representative of the Adversary has therefore these powers committed unto him -- partly because it was through them that such powers prevailed against Job, and partly because these powers did really become Satan, that is adversaries, to Job, and if no other adversaries had been concerned there would have been elegance, but no impropriety, in giving them an active representative. This is nothing more than a personification of inanimate or latent powers, and is very common with the best writers both ancient and modern. Upon the whole, there is no reason to believe, that the word Satan is ever used in the old Testament, to denote a fallen angel, or a real, evil, separate spirit;

---

[55] Compare Zech. iii. with Ezra v.
[56] See Isaiah, Chap. xiv. and Ezekiel Chap. xvi. also the Lamentations of Jeremiah, &c.

but there are good reasons to believe the contrary, for it is clearly proved in many instances.

FINIS.

AN ATTEMPT TO PROVE
THAT THE OPINION CONCERNING
THE DEVIL, OR SATAN, AS A FALLEN ANGEL,
AND THAT HE TEMPTS MEN TO SIN, HATH NO
REAL FOUNDATION IN SCRIPTURE.

BEING A SUPPLEMENT

to a

PAMPHLET PUBLISHED ABOUT THE YEAR 1770,

ENTITLED,

AN ENQUIRY INTO THE SCRIPTURE MEANING OF THE WORD SATAN.

The SECOND EDITION,

with considerable Additions.

By WM. ASHDOWNE.

"Time, that destroys the fictions of error and opinion, confirms the determinations of nature, and of truth."

-- CICERO of the nature of the Gods.

Section I

AN ATTEMPT, &c. SECT I. An Examination of the Passages in the Old Testament, in which the Words DEVILS and SATAN occur, and what is related of him.

THE first text in which the former word is mentioned is, Liv. xvii. 7. And they shall no more offer their sacrifices unto Devils, after whom they have gone a whoring. --That by Devils is meant, the idols or objects of idolatry only, is plain, from Deut. xxxii. 16, 17. They (the Israelites) provoked God to jealousy with their strange gods; they sacrificed unto Devils,[57] not to God; to gods whom they knew not; to new gods that came newly up, whom your fathers feared not. Of Jeroboam, it is related, 2 Chron. xi. 15. That he ordained him priests for the high places, and for the Devils, and for the calves which he had made. --They sacrificed to the calves, I Kings, xii. 31, 32. He made other gods and molten images to provoke God to anger. xiv. 9. In Psal. cvi. 35. 38, it is related of the people of Israel, when they were mingled with the Heathen, and learned their works, That they served their idols, which was snare unto them; yea, they sacrificed their sons and their daughters unto Devils, i.e. to the idols of Canaan. Of the Heathen, the Apostle saith, The things which the Gentiles sacrifice, they sacrifice to Devils; and I would not that ye should have fellowship with Devils. I Cor. x. 20. viii. 7. 10. Deut. xii. 30, 31. Rev. ix. 20. The first text in which the word Satan occurs, in our translation, is, I Chron. xxi. I. And Satan stood up against Israel, and provoked (or moved David, as the same original word is rendered in the next verse) to number Israel; or, as it is worded, 2 Sam. xxiv. I, Again the anger of the Lord was kindled against

---

[57] Dr. Taylor, in his Hebrew Concordance, saith, "It signifies hairy, or a goat, so called from its shaggy hair. The deities worshipped, in Egypt, such as oxen, dogs, wolves, monkeys, goats." It may just be observed, that the word Devil doth not once occur in the Old Testament.

Israel, and he moved David against them to say, Go, number Israel and Judah.⁵⁸ Whenever the people were numbered, from twenty years old and upwards, each one, whether rich or poor, is commanded to pay half a shekel, Exod. xxx. II, &c. This was to be applied to the service of the tabernacle of the congregation, that it may be a memorial unto the children of Israel before the Lord, to make an atonement for their souls. But there is not even the least hint in either of the fore-cited chapters, that David intended, or gave any order to Joab to collect the half shekel of the people that were numbered. And it is plain, that Joab, his chief General, looked upon the King's command as abominable; and said to him "Why doth my Lord require this thing? Why will he be a cause of trespass to Israel?" And when he and the inferior officers had executed the King's command, at least in part, and returned to him with the list of the men, it appears plain he very soon recollected he had trespassed by not observing the command of God, in Exodus. I Chron. xxi. 8. In his confession, mentioned in this chapter, it doth not in the least appear, he perceived in himself that he was tempted by Satan to commit the sin, or that he was moved to it by God; and indeed, as God charged him with the sin, or transgression, we cannot suffer ourselves to admit he was either the sole or partial cause of it.⁵⁹ From David's opposing

---

⁵⁸ Mr. Farmer observes, in his Answer to Dr. Worthington, p. 53, That the authors of the Septuagint did not imagine there were any reference to Satan in I Chron. xxi. i. which they render και ανεςη διαβολος (not Diabolos εν τω ισραελ and there arose an enemy in Israel. Even in reference to a good angel, the Hebrew word is translated (text illegible) by the Septuagint, Numb. xxii. 32. which therefore must denote opposition without malice. In reference to the same angel, the Septuagint uses the verb from which (text illegible) is derived.

⁵⁹ Though the original word translated "moved," doth in most texts where it occurs, properly signify stirred up, persuaded, or enticed by the influence which one person hath over or upon another, to engage him to act conformable thereto, as appears in these texts, Deut. xiii. 6, 7. Joshua xv. 18. I Kings xxi. 25. 2 Chron. xviii. 2. yet it cannot well be admitted in the case under consideration, for as the Apostle James saith,

Joab's judgment and remonstrance against numbering the people, it is evident he was determined upon it from whatever cause it arose. Farther, it appears from Samuel, just cited, that previous to this, Israel, or the people had sinned, and it provoked God; for, it is said, Again the anger of the Lord was kindled against Israel. What their former sin was, is not mentioned; but for that, as well as for their present transgression, God punished the people; as is related, 2 Sam. xxiv. 11, &c. David again confessed, that as he alone had sinned, he and and his family only deserved to be punished.

Finally, I observe, that in the sacred writings extant, prior to the writing the book of Chronicles, there is not the least mention of any angel being cast out of Heaven on account of his having sinned against God, as the common opinion of such an apostate spirit; and therefore the writer of it, by the word Satan, could not intend such a being. Indeed, had any of those writers made mention of such a being, and that he had tempted or provoked any of the people to sin by his secret wiles or suggestions, there would then be some plausible ground to suppose that Satan provoked David to number the people: but it is certain they have not, even in a single instance. The Satan, or adversary, that excited him to undertake it, probably was his pride, or some other inordinate or criminal desire; or perhaps, the fear of a formidable enemy. One or other of these, it is probable, led him to overrule the better judgment and expostulation of Joab, who was entirely against it. That it was his act only, is plain, from his own words. I Chron. xxi. 8. 17. The next text where the word Satan occurs, is in Job. i. 8. and ii. 1. 2. That a fallen angel, or a wicked apostate spirit is not meant, appears to me, at least highly probable, from the following considerations: One is, it is very incredible that the Lord should hold the conversation there related, with such a being, and also that he should give him leave to afflict his pious servant with the sore disorder of the boils merely to gratify the groundless and invidious insinuation or charge of such a wicked

---

As God cannot be tempted with evil, neither tempted he any man. i. e. by any real influence on his mind to excite him to do that which is evil.

spirit; that his serving God was not from a pious and good principle, but because he had blessed him with an abundance; but, that if he endangered his life, he would rebel against him. In either view of this relation, it certainly is without any precedent in all the Bible; and, I own, I cannot reconcile the latter part with the many declarations in those very writings in which is expressed God's regard to those that serve him, in like manner as is related of Job's piety to God; his paternal regard for his children's religious welfare and happiness; and his acts of beneficence manifested to the necessitous, related in chap. xxix. That neither Job, nor his wife believed the boils were inflicted by Satan, as a wicked spirit, but by the hand of God, is plain, from chap. ii. 9, 10. and from chap. i. 21. it is equally plain he believed that his other afflictions came upon him from God; and from the speeches of his friends, it is alike evident that they understood all his afflictions came upon him by the appointment of God; and after the Lord had blessed him with a double portion of goods, as chap. xlii. 10, 11. it is said, Then came there unto him, all his brethren and all his sisters, and all they that had been of his acquaintance before, and they bemoaned over him all the evils that the Lord bad brought upon him; and, according to the custom of that time, and what is similar with it at present in the Eastern countries, every man also gave him a piece of money, and, every one an earring of gold. Lastly, I observe in all that is related of Satan, respecting Job, there is not the least intimation of his infusing into his mind evil thoughts, or exciting in him any inordinate desires, by which he tempted him to sin against the Lord, either prior to, or after he was afflicted with the boils. The next text in which the word Satan is mentioned is, Zach. iii. 1, &c. The first six chapters appear to contain a revelation by a vision made to the prophet concerning the Israelites, upon their return from the Babylonian captivity, and their building the Temple; and the principal persons that are mentioned are Joshua and Zerubbabel.

This appears highly probable by consulting the time when the prophet lived and prophesied, and comparing what he says in the context, we are considering with what is related. Ezra v. Then the prophets Haggai, and Zachariah the son of Iddo, prophesied unto the Jews that were in Judea and Jerusalem, in the name of the God of Israel, even unto them. Then rose up Zerubbabel the son of Shealtiel, and Jeshua the son of Joszadak, and began to build the house of God which is at Jerusalem, and with them were the prophets of God helping them: i. e. by their prophesying. Their adversaries are thus described: At that time came to them Tatnai, Governor on this side the river; and Shether-boznai, and their companions, and said thus to them: Who hath commanded you to build the house and make the walls? Then said we unto them, after this manner; What are the names of the men that make this building? In short, they would have made them desist from building, and wrote to Darius for that purpose; but it stands recorded thus: The eyes of the Lord were upon the elders of the Jews, so that they, (their adversaries, or Satan) could not cause them to cease till the affair came before Darius, who made a decree, that they should not only suffer the building to go on, but also assist the builders with such things as might be needful. Another text in which the word Satan occurs, is, Psal. cix. 6. Set thou a wicked man over him, (i. e. mine enemy) and let Satan stand at his right hand.[60] It is exceeding plain that in the context David is speaking of men who were his enemies, he saith, "For my love, they are my adversaries." But the Hebrew word rendered adversaries, and also in the verses 20, 29, is the same as in verse 6, translated Satan.[61] Had the word in the former verses been translated as in the latter, it would be, They are my Satans. But, I judge, there is no discerning man who can believe that the persons he had mentioned as the wicked, who encompassed him about with words of hatred, and fought against him, were fallen angels, but men only. Besides the foregoing texts where the words Devils and Satan occur, there are others wherein mention is made of an

---

[60] On this verse Dr. Patrick comments, Let the worst man that can be found be appointed to hear his cause when he is accused, and his most malicious adversary plead against him.
[61] See Taylor's Hebrew Concordance, No. 1928.

evil spirit, that, by some persons, may be interpreted and understood to intend a fallen angel, and therefore be urged against what I have asserted respecting the entire silence of those writings concerning such a being. These texts will be considered, and the first I will produce is, I Kings, xxii. 21, 22, 23.[62] The occasion of the Prophet's mentioning the vision, is related in the foregoing verses, which need not be cited. The vision will be easily discerned, and also allowed to be not a relation of a fact, which then took place, but only a representation made to the Prophet relative to Ahab and Jehoshaphat's going to besiege Ramoth Gilead. Farther, it appears to me highly improbable, at least, that the Prophet believed, the spirit said, to come forth, or out from among the good angels, who are represented as standing before the throne of God, was intended to represent a fallen angel, or apostate spirit; and, I think it will appear in that light to every one who attends to the passage. I judge it will also be granted to have been equally improbable to the Prophet, that God should send such a being to execute the message there related. That which, in my opinion, is an unanswerably strong and decided proof of the justness of the foregoing observations, respecting the Prophet's opinion of the evil spirit not being a fallen angel, is the entire silence of the Scriptures, that such a being had been cast out of Heaven, as I have already observed; and it is past doubt, that in the vision there is not the least hint that the evil spirit was a representation of one of them. If it is admitted the vision was subsequent to what is related of the 400 prophets who prophesied to Ahab and Jehoshaphat, that success would attend their besieging Ramoth Gilead, it is plain, that the former was already persuaded of the truth of their prediction,

---

[62] And there came forth a spirit and stood before the Lord, and said, I will persuade him, i. e. Ahab. And the Lord said, wherewith? And he said I will go forth and will be a lying spirit in the mouth of all his prophets; and he said, thou shalt persuade and prevail also, go forth and do so. Now therefore behold the Lord hath put a lying spirit in the mouth of all these thy prophets, and the Lord hath spoken evil concerning thee.

particularly by what is said of Zedekiah and the other prophets, v. 11, 12. But supposing it should be granted that the evil spirit who came forth and offered to go and persuade Ahab represents a fallen angel, yet it will not prove there is more than one. I may still add, that whoever will be at the pains to look at the numerous texts in the Old Testament, particularly in Jeremiah and Ezekiel, wherein mention is made of the false prophets, will not find the least hint that they were stirred up, or excited to prophesy falsely, and thereby deceive the people, by an evil spirit, i. e. a fallen angel. But those writings have assigned very different and apparent causes, from whence they were induced or excited to deceive the people by their prophesying false things, as the prophets did we have mentioned.

On the whole, there doth not seem to be the least proof that the evil spirit, mentioned in the vision, was designed to represent a fallen angel; or was so understood by the prophet to whom it appeared. Another text I shall taken under consideration, is, I Sam. xvi. 14,[63] &c. Previous to my offering any observations upon it, I judge it will be proper to attend to what is related in chapter the tenth, wherein mention is made of God's sending Samuel to choose Saul, and anoint him to be King over his people. To whom Samuel said, The spirit of the Lord will come upon thee, and thou shalt prophesy, and thou shalt be turned into another man: And after he had turned back from him, God gave him another heart; and when he and his companions came to the hill, a company of the prophets met him, and the spirit of God came upon him, and he prophesied among them. Sometime after this, God, by Samuel, sent him to go up against Amalick, and utterly destroyed it; as it is related chapter xi. but, instead of his fully executing this commission, he spared Agag, &c. as v. 8, 9. Upon this, Samuel came to him, and, among other things. plainly told him, as v. 22, 23, that, for this act of perverse disobedience, God rejected him from being King. Soon after this, Samuel was sent to anoint David, the son of Jesse, to be King in his stead, which he

---

[63] The spirit of the Lord departed from Saul, and an evil spirit, from the Lord, troubled him.

accordingly did; tho' the commencement of his reign did not take place till the death of Saul. I think there can hardly be any doubt that Saul was informed of David's being anointed King. Let any one, for a moment, only consider these particular cases, which, it is natural to believe, very deeply affected the mind of Saul: It was imbittered with the just accusation of his own inexcusable guilt; or, in the words of Samuel to him: Rebellion is as the sin of witchcraft, and stubbornness is as iniquity and idolatry; thou hast rejected the word of the Lord in not executing it on the Amaelkites. That God, who had raised him up in a very singular manner to be the first King over his people Israel; that he had with-drawn his spirit from him by which he had prophesied among the prophets; and, finally, he had, by a special direction to Samuel, anointed David to be King; and to him he had given his spirit. A proper attention to these very interesting particulars, will, I presume, without any difficulty, explain in what sense we are to understand that an evil spirit from the Lord troubled him; and also the true cause from whence his servants, who, no doubt, saw his unusual dejection of mind, said to him, Behold! now, an evil spirit, from God, troubleth thee. To remove, or mitigate which, they gave him this advice: Let our Lord the King command thy servants to seek out a man who is a cunning player on a harp, and it shall come to pass, when the evil spirit, from God, is upon thee, that he will play with his hand, and thou shalt be well. To which proposal he assented; and David was sent for; and when the evil spirit, from God, was upon Saul, he took an harp and played with his hand: So Saul was refreshed, and was well, and the evil spirit departed from him.--The success attending the advice of his servants, shews plainly what was their opinion of the real cause, as well as the nature of his trouble. I presume it will be allowed there is not the least evidence in the context from whence we may justly suppose, that Saul's servants believed the power of the musical harp could possibly expel a fallen angel from Saul, had they understood it to be such a being. But it was not an improper expedient to relieve his mind, under its present disordered state; especially if we may suppese that he was rather fond of that kind of music. Men, in common, and even very sensible men too, through the force of habit, are very apt to affix to the words evil spirit, they find in Scripture, the idea of a fallen angel; and then incautiously conclude that those writers used them in the same sense; but this is often, as in the case before us, a very capital error, as, I presume, will appear more fully in the following pages. There is another text in Judges chapter ix. 23. where it is said, God sent an evil spirit between Abimelech and the men of Shechem. After the death of Gideon, the father of Abimelech, he applied to the men of Shechem to obtain their consent, that, as one of his sons, he might rule over them in his stead; but that he might not have any competitor in the family of Jerubbaal his brother, who had sixty sons, he obtained money out of the house of Baal-berith, with which he hired vain and light persons, and by these he slew them all, except Jotham, the youngest, who escaped from that unnatural and unprovoked massacre. Upon this, the Shechemites made him King. As they in general were not concerned in that wicked act, Jotham addressed them to retaliate it upon Abimelech and those who were concerned with him; as v. 7--20. After Abimelech had reigned three years, it is said God sent an evil spirit, &c. I think it is probable that the Shechemites, who were not concerned with him, in consequence of Jotham's expostulation, meditated revenge against him and his adherents, and therefore commenced hostilities against him; upon which Abimilech, with his forces, went against Shechem, and slew many of the people; after which he attacked Thebez, and took it; but, upon his attempt upon the tower, he was slain. Upon his death, it is said, verses 56, 57, Thus God rendered the wickedness of Abimelech, which he did unto his father, in slaying his brethren; and for all the evil of the men of Shechem did God render upon their heads, and upon them came the curses of Jotham, the son of Jerubbaal. From this relation, it appears plain, to me, that by an evil spirit is not to be understood a fallen angel; but, that God, in the course of his Providence, raised, or stirred up an enemy to Abimelech and his adherents: as, verses 56, 57. to punish them for the wicked act of slaying the sons of Jerubbaal his brother, who had rendered signal services to his people against their enemies in the time of Gideon their father. Another text is in Psalms lviii. 49, where, it is said, God cast upon them (the Egyptians) the fierceness of his wrath and indignation, by sending evil angels. I would just observe that the Hebrew word here rendered angels, is often and justly translated Messengers, and sometimes Prophets, who, from God, delivered his messages to his people; and therefore the word Angels, doth, by no means, always intend angels as invisible spirits, much less fallen angels. This can be determined only by the context, or parallel passages. Now, it is indisputably, plain, in the context, the writer gives a summary account of God's dealings with the Egyptians, as is particularly recorded in Exod. vii. to the xiii. But, it is certain, that Moses hath not mentioned evil angels being sent among the Egyptians. The only angels, or messengers he hath related whom God sent among them, were himself and Aaron, by whose instrumentality God cast upon them the fierceness of his wrath, &c. and in this sense, to the Egyptians they were evil angels, or messengers. Now, I think, it will be granted, that the Psalmist could not derive any knowledge of evil angels, i. e. apostate spirits, being sent among the people of Egypt, but from the History of Moses, in which there is not even any hint of such beings sent among them. I here beg leave to observe, that whatever real knowledge men have of angels, i. e. their intellectual powers, or their visible communications with men, or their being the agents of God in his providential government in this world, that it is wholly derived from divine revelation, without which it is absolutely impossible they can have the least knowledge of either; and the reason is as obvious as it is unquestionably true, viz. because they are the inhabitants of the invisible world. And this is equally true, as it respects any of those beings having sinned against God, and on that account expelled from Heaven. But, even supposing that was clearly revealed, yet that would be no proof of their tempting men to sin, by suggesting to their minds evil thoughts, or raising in them corrupt desires, terminating in sinful actions. A real knowledge of these things must depend upon revelation, or a relation of real facts in proof of it. But of these things the Old Testament is entirely silent, as we have seen.[64] Thus much concerning what we find in the Old Testament.

---

[64] Mr. Farmer's opinion is this,--That the Old Testament contains no account of the fall of angels, much less does it represent them as scaling Heaven, and being thrown down from thence. There is not even the most distant reference, or allusion to such an event in any of the Jewish prophets. Farther, he saith, I am far from taking upon me to say there was not an early revelation of the rebellion of angels, and their expulsion from Heaven. But hitherto this point has been asserted only,-- not proved.

Section 2

SECT. II. I will now examine the New Testament to see whether any thing occurs therein to corroborate the commonly received opinion of Fallen Angels, or Satan and the Devil.

THE only texts, or at least the principal ones, are, in I Pet. ii. 4. and Jude v. 6. For if God spared not the angels that sinned, but cast them down to Hell, and delivered them into chains of darkness to be reserved unto judgment. And the angels which kept not their first estate, but left their own habitations, he hath reserved in everlasting chains of darkness unto the judgment of the great day. On these words I observe, first, That none of the Apostles could derive the least knowledge from the Old Testament, that any of the angels had been cast out of Heaven on account of their having sinned against God; and we have no account that Jesus made any discovery of it to them. Secondly, Had Peter, or Jude, known, from the Old Testament, or from Jesus, that there were fallen angels, it is natural to suppose they would have been explicit in mentioning them to the persons they wrote to, otherwise they could not have understood what beings they intended; and that for reasons already offered. Thirdly, Neither of the particulars just mentioned, can be satisfactorily inferred from the word Angels. The primary import of the original word is, to relate any matter, particularly as a messenger, and in this sense, the same original word is rendered, James ii. 25. These messengers were sent to spy the interior parts of the land of Canaan; and, upon their return, they related to Moses and to the people what they had seen and heard in traversing it. And there is but one text where the original word can in the least be supposed to allude to fallen angels, and that is Matt. xxv. 41. Fourthly, That the word[65], translated cast down to Hell, is the only place in the New Testament where it is translated cast down

---

[65] ταρταρυω

to Hell. Fifthly, All that the two Apostles have related of the conduct of the angels, is, that they sinned, and kept not their first estate, or principality, but left (not were cast out of) their own habitation; where that was is not mentioned. Of the punishment, it is said they were cast down to Hell, and delivered into chains of darkness to be reserved unto judgment of the great day. But there is not the least mention what their sinful conduct was, nor that they were cast out of Heaven and separated from the good angels. Let us now see whether the context in Peter favors the commonly received opinion or not. In the foregoing chapters he saith to his brethren, that he and the apostles who were with the Lord on the Mount, Matt. xvii. 1, &c. heard a voice from Heaven, saying, this is my beloved Son, in whom I am well pleased. He then adds, That we have a more sure word of prophesy, i. e. a more particular and full revelation in the Old Testament concerning Jesus as the Son of God, which ye will do well to give heed to, because those writings were indited by the Holy Ghost; and the meaning of those parts of them, respecting Jesus, are not confined to the prophets, or that people; but we also are included therein: And then he tells them, that in the time of those prophets, there were false ones among that people; and there are, or will arise, false teachers among you, who will propagate false doctrines, even denying the Lord that bought them, and draw away many after them, and thereby bring upon themselves swift destruction. And he describes the way or manner by which they will attempt to draw them away. And from v. 10--19, I think he represents their principle and conduct; and against such false prophets Jesus warned his disciples, Matt. vii. 15. 26. 29. xxiv. 11. Mark xiii. 21, 22, 23. See Acts xx. 30. And I apprehend the Apostle St. John alluded to such persons. I Epistle, iv. 1, 2, 3, calling them Anti-Christs, i. e. opposers or enemies of Christ. In the chapter under consideration, the Apostle warns the Christians to be aware of them that they might not fall under the same condemnation which would overtake those false teachers. And in verse 4, he mentions others, whom he calls angels, or messengers that sinned, &c. The opinion of a very sensible anonymous author[66] on this subject, appears to me at least very probable, that the angels, i. e. the messengers that sinned, are those men related Numb. xiii. xiv. who were sent to spy out the land of Canaan, whose report to Moses, &c. of the numbers and situation of some of its inhabitants, and the strength of their cities, discouraged the people from going up to take possession of it. These were rulers and heads of the people whom God punished for giving such an account, by inflicting on them a great plague, so that they and all the people whom they caused to murmur against God, and Moses his servant, died. Heb. iii. 7. 19. Both the messengers and the people had seen the mighty power of God exerted in their deliverances and yet they did not believe, but rebelled. Those messengers who sinned, were plain and pertinent examples of men like themselves, from whom they might and ought to take warning not to be seduced by the false teachers, and thereby be guilty of a like unbelief, i. e. in Jesus their Lord, and a wicked departure from his commands, which, from conviction they had embraced, and on that account, fall under an heavier condemnation and judgment from God, than he had inflicted on those messengers and the people seduced by them. But, I apprehend, that if we understand the passage we are commenting upon, of fallen angels, it was neither applicable, nor indeed intelligible to the apostles, or the people to whom he was writing, since they had no knowledge that any of the angels had sinned, or wherein it consisted; and, I may add, if they had, what was the conduct of angels, (properly such) to them? The other instances are clearly taken from men like themselves; the probability therefore is, that these were of the same nature with those, who, in the time of Noah, God drowned by a deluge; and then he introduces the similar conduct of the inhabitants of Sodom, &c. whom God destroyed by fire. But, as a contrast to these, he mentions the cases of Noah and Lot, who believed in God, and

---

[66] An Enquiry into the Scripture meaning of the word Satan.

obeyed his word, and were saved from those judgments. These, and the former persons, were obvious examples of men of the like passions with themselves, which they could not only easily understand, but also easily apply the former as warnings, and the latter as encouragements to fortify their minds against those false teachers; but, I apprehend, they could not, as it respected fallen angels.

What force these observations will be admitted to have, as proofs, that by the word Angels that finned, &c. the Apostle did not intend fallen angels, but the rulers and heads of the people, mentioned above, is submitted to the deliberate and unbiassed judgment of the reader. In the preceding quotations from the Old Testament, where the words Devils and Satan, &c. occur, it appears to me, there is not any proof that the writers in using them, meant fallen angels; and therefore they do not give the least account that Satan, in a secret or unperceived manner, infused, or put into the mind or heart of any one man, evil thoughts, or excited in him inordinate desires, by which he tempted him to sin. Likewise, in the New Testament it appears, that there is not any explicit relation that any of the angels were expelled Heaven for their having sinned against God. It will therefore follow, that in the former writings in which it is recorded of individuals, or of the people in general who sinned against God by violating the obligations of natural or revealed religion, or both; they have not, even in a single instance, attributed to the temptation of Satan. In this they are as entirely silent as they are respecting any man's being possessed by one of them, or by a demon; and yet had Satan been the real agent, or instrument in tempting men to sin in like manner; or, as universally as it is now believed he doth, I think it will be allowed to be natural to expect the writers of the Old Teftament would have given some plain account of it, in some instances; for it is certain they repeatedly mention many different causes or occasions from whence men were tempted to sin; but, it is certain, they have not attributed it to Satan in a single instance. From those writings therefore it seems to be indisputably certain, that neither the Apostles nor the Jews could derive the least information concerning Satan or his devices; or, that any person, much less men in general, had been tempted by him to sin. Should it be said, that the relation given of the Serpent's tempting Eve, and seducing her to sin, is a proof that an individual at least, is an exception; I answer, that, admitting it was by a fallen angel who assumed the bodily shape of that creature, or entered into one, (of which however there is not the least mention in the Bible) yet the relation of his tempting her was, by conversing with her, and not by his infusing in an invisible or unperceived manner into her mind or heart, evil thoughts, or raising evil desires in her, as is now believed to be the way or manner by which he tempts men to sin; consequently the former essentially differs from the latter. And, I suppose there is not any man who will plead that Satan tempts men after that manner. Her being tempted, as is related, I should therefore apprehend cannot justly be urged as a real or satisfactory proof of Satan's tempting men to sin. In what conspicuous light must the difference appear between the sacred writings and those of other men in the present and past ages who lived under the light of the Christian religion, which are replete with assertions that a fallen angel assumed the shape of a real serpent, or entered into one; and that he tempted her and her posterity to the commission of the sins which they have been guilty of, or at least, to the principal part of them. But was the commonly received opinion that it was a fallen angel entered into the serpent, proved to be justly founded in the plain language of Scripture, which it certainly is not, yet that could not prove there is more than one as a tempter of men to sin? And, I may justly remark, there is not even a single text in the New Testament where the word Devils is to be found. The only one from whence it may seem to be inferred is, Matt. xxv. 41. where Jesus spoke of the Devil and his angels. For, in every other text where the word Devils occurs, it it is Daimonia, and not Diabolos. The only text where the last word hath a plural meaning is, I Tim. iii. 11. 2 Epistle iii. 3. Titus ii. 3. and is rendered slanderers and accusers. Likewise wherever the word Satan is mentioned in the New Testament, except Matt. xii. 26. it is in the singular only, and there it can include two Satans only; also where the words the Prince of this world, the Prince of the power of the air, occur, it is in the singular only. The same is true of the words, the Power of Darkness. When in Luke xi. 18. Jesus repeating what the Jews said of him, that he cast out Devils; the original word is Diamonia, a word of very different signification from Diabolos, or Satanas. If the common opinion that there are numerous Satans, or Devils, is pleaded for, it certainly cannot be proved from any expressions either in the New Testament or in the Old; because those writings invariably use the word Devil, or Satan, in the singular, and never in the plural number as importing there are many such beings; and I will just note, that in all the conversations the Jews had with Jesus, they do not even once make use of the words Diabolos, i. e. Devil, or Satanas. The first relation, in the New Testament, of Satan, or the Devil tempting any one, is that of Jesus. Matt. iv. I--II. Mark i. 11, 12. Luke iv. 1--13. Matthew and Luke relate, he was led up of the spirit into the Wilderness to be tempted of the Devil, and mark that the spirit driveth him into the Wilderness; and when he had fasted forty days and forty nights, he was afterwards an hungred. The particulars related of Satan's tempting Jesus is, his saying, If thou be the Son of God, command that these stones be made bread; i. e. to supply you with food. His taking him up upon a pinnacle or battlement of the Temple, and saying to him, If thou be the Son of God, cast thyself down from hence, for it is written, he, (i. e. God) shall give his angels charge concerning thee; and in their hands they shall hold thee up, lest, at any time, thou dash thy foot against a stone. His taking him up on an exceeding high mountain, and shewing him all the kingdoms of the world, and the glory of them; and saying, All these things will I give thee, and the glory of them, if thou wilt fall down and worship me; for they are delivered unto me, and to whomsoever I will I give it. I would just premise, that a person may be said to be tempted when an offer is made of what is agreeable to him, or when it excites in him some desire to accept of it; or when, as the apostle James saith, he is tempted, being drawn away of his own lust, and enticed, and thereby it bringeth forth sin. Now, suppose it is admitteed that Satan is a fallen angel, and that what he said to Jesus is to be literally understood; yet, I think it cannot be doubted but he knew who he was, and his design and end in tempting him. I should therefore judge that no man can really believe the proposals were agreeable to him, much less that they raised in him a desire to comply with either of them; and, as to the last, it is certain, that both Satan and Jesus well knew it was not in Satan's power to give him them had Jesus complied with the condition. On what real ground then can it be justly supposed, that if Satan knew he was the Son of God, he could have the least reason to believe or expect he could tempt him to comply with either proposal. Indeed, if we may judge of this temptation as a true specimen of the artful wiles of Satan, (I mean if there is such a being) it certainly doth not evidence his abilities in tempting men to be superior to those of men; or, that he is a much more subtle and powerful tempter; for, had he, in either of those respects, been superior to men, I think we may justly conclude, that his tempting Jesus would have been much more artfully laid and conducted, and therefore more likely to have succeeded than in what is related by the Evangelists. I would finally observe, they have not given the least intimation, that Satan, in an invisible manner, unperceived by Jesus, infused into his mind any evil thoughts, or raised in him any inordinate desires to tempt him, as the means by which most men believe he tempts persons to sin. The next relation of the Devil, or Satan's tempting, I will mention, is that of Judas. John xiii. 2. 27. it is said, That, supper being ended, the Devil now put into the head of Judas Iscariot to betray Jesus; or, that after supper he gave him the sop, when Satan entered into him. When he had taken it, he immediately went out, or he went his way, and communed with the chief priests, and said to them, What will ye give me, and I will deliver him unto you? And they were glad, and covenanted with him for thirty pieces of silver, and he promised and sought opportunity to betray him unto them in the absence of the multitude. Luke xxii. 3--6. I must again intreat the reader to consider, that neither John nor Luke could have received, from the Old Testament, the least knowledge of Satan as a fallen angel, or of his having put into the heart of any man evil thoughts, by which he tempted him to sin; or, that he ever entered into any one to effect it. Neither is there any proof, in the evangelists, that they had received from Jesus the last knowledge of either; and, and indeed, this is the only account, in the Bible, of Satan's having entered into any man. For all the instances recorded in the New Testament of men's being possessed by an evil spirit, or spirits, are, of a demon, or demons, and not by Satan as a fallen angel. Farther, I observe that in every passage in the Evangelists in which Jesus mentioned to his apostles, or to Judas, his being betrayed by one of them, he did not give them the least intimation that he would be tempted to it by Satan, much less by his entering into him as the real cause of it. If we impartially attend to what John has related of his principle and conduct, chap. xii. 6. that he cared not for the poor, and being purse-bearer, he used to pilfer what was in bank; as the original words are rendered by another translator: and likewise that Jesus said he is a devil, i. e. an adversary or accuser, and not clean, like the rest of the apostles; xiii. 11. and his covenanting with the chief priests for thirty pieces of silver, to betray him. It is probable we shall be led to understand John's and Luke's words, cited above, not in the literal sense, but only as expressive of Judas's principle and conduct as a very covetous man and an adversary to Jesus, who was then going to execute his design; and it is reasonable to believe, he previously knew the chief priests had sought to take and destroy Jesus. Luke says, Judas sought to betray him unto them, in the absence of the multitude, and therefore he came in the night, with the officers, to take him: and the Evangelists have related that the chief priests, &c. before that time had attempted to take him, but they did not, fearing the people. How far these observations may be admitted to explain and also to ascertain the true meaning of the words under consideration, is submitted to the judgment of the inquisitive and candid reader. In my view, they appear the most probable salutation of them; at least the literal meaning seems to be attended with considerable, if not with insuperable dissiculties, especially that of Satan's entering into Judas. The next account of Satan I will mention, is that respecting Peter. Luke xxii. 31, 32. Jesus said to him, Satan hath desired to have you, that he may sift you as wheat, i. e. separate you from me, like as that grain is from the chaff, not to be united to me again. But he added, I have prayed for thee, that thy faith fail not, i. e. in producing a final separation from me; understanding literally, that Satan desired to have Peter for the purpose expressed in the text, it is very natural to ask to whom it was communicated? I presume we cannot well suppose it was to Jesus, because, prior to any effect it could have upon Peter, Jesus had prayed for him that his faith might not fail him in the sense just mentioned. If Satan's desire was not divulged, it could operate only in himself; but if it excited him to sift Peter, yet his Lord's praying for him would render his tempting him as ineffectual as what is related of his tempting Jesus; and if, as is generally believed, that Satan knows the thoughts and actions of men, he could not but know of Jesus's interposing in favor of his favorite disciple, and therefore that any attempt upon him must prove abortive.

That Peter's faith failed him to a great degree, is manifest in the Evangelists: but, in attending to what they have related as the apparent cause, or occasion of it, we shall plainly discern it arose from a different adversary than Satan; that is, from his own natural fear of being involved as a disciple of Jesus in the condemnation, &c. which he saw it was very probable would befall him from the hatred of the high priests, &c. against him when he was present at his trial, and heard him accused of being a malefactor and seditious person, and likewise charged with having designs against Cæsar's government, by assuming to himself the title of King of the Jews, and himself openly accused as an accomplice with Jesus. This view of the cause of Peter's faith failing him, clearly explains and accounts for it as the adversary or Satan that occasioned it. If Satan was the real cause of his faith failing him, it must be attributed to his exciting his fear lest he should suffer with Jesus; but of this there is not the least intimation in either of the evangelists, nor as it respects the rest of the apostles, who, as well as he, said, they would not deny him even unto death; but it is plain their faith failed them as well as Peter's. That which is peculiar to him is, his thrice denying him at his trial, as is particularly related. And it is evident the evangelists have not given the least hint that Satan stirred up or tempted the high priests, &c. to act the part they did to Jesus, that occasioned Peter's fear, and which led him to deny his Lord. The true and apparent causes or occasions of the high priests, &c. proceedings against Jesus are clearly related by the evangelists, and which began to take place long before his trial; for prior to that time the Pharisees, &c. on several occasions attempted to take him and put him to death, as is related in their writings. I may farther observe, that in every text in which is related Jesus told his disciples, or Peter in particular, that they would deny him thro' the weakness of their faith, alluding to the time when it took place; he did not give them the least hint it would arise from the instigation of Satan on their mind. They could not have any real ground to believe this, because, as I have observed, there is not the least proof, either in the Old Testament, or the words of Jesus, so far as we are capable of judging, from which they could know there was a fallen angel, or that he tempted men to sin. Having attempted to explain the passages wherein are related Satan's tempting Jesus and the two apostles, I will crave the reader's attention to what our Lord said in some of his parables of the wicked one, Satan, or the Devil, as tempting men; and the first instance is that of the sower who sowed the good seed in his field. Matt, xiii. Mark iv. Luke vii. of the seed that was sown by the highway, he said, When one heared the word of the kingdom and understandeth it not, or hath not an honest and good heart, then cometh the wicked one and catcheth or taketh away that which was sown in his heart; or when they have heard, Satan cometh immediately and taketh away the word that was sown in their hearts. Satan's tempting these persons is represented to be his taking away the word out of their heart; but not by his instilling, or putting into it evil thoughts, or raising in it evil desires. And it is unquestionably certain, that the above account differs from all other instances related in the New Testament, where he is said to tempt men. The persons above described in the parable, I think are plainly alluded to, and represented verses 13, 14, 15, as dull of hearing, having closed their eyes, lest at any time they should see with their eyes, and hear with their ears, and should understand with their heart, and should be converted, and I should heal them; which plainly accounts for the word that was sown in their hearts not abiding there. In the parable of the man who made a great supper, Luke xiv. 15, &c. as somewhat similar in our Lord's intention with that just considered; he hath explicitly assigned other and very different causes why the persons invited to it did not accept of the invitation than that of Satan's tempting them: They are these, They all began to make excuse; the first said, I have bought a piece of ground, and I must needs go and see it; I pray thee have me excused. -- And another said, I have bought five yoke of oxen, and I go to prove them; I pray thee have me excused. -- And another said, I have married a wife, and therefore I cannot come. So the servant came and shewed his lord all these things. These causes why the word did not abide in their hearr, are similar with those Jesus assigned why the seed that was sown on stony ground, and on that where the thorns grew up and choaked it, viz. when tribulation ariseth, because of the word, and by and by they are offended; or the care of this world and the deceitfulness of riches, and the lusts of other things, and pleasures of this life, enter in and choak the word, and he beareth no fruit. These obvious and usual occasions of temptation to the persons represented in those parables, the people present could easily understand, and also apply it usefully to themselves; but they could not as it respects the secret suggestions of Satan, or the Devil.

 And, in the course of Jesus's Ministry, he mentioned many other causes why men did not receive the word than in those parables, as must be obvious to every one who reads with attention his discourses to the people who attended him. Thus, when he said to some of the unbelieving Jews. -- How can ye believe, which receive honour one of another, and seek not the honour that cometh from God only? I will just subjoin the following texts, in which he hath particularly mentioned several other evident causes of men's being tempted not to receive the word, that may be compared to those represented by the highway, without giving the least intimation of the wicked one taking away the word out of their heart. Luke xiii. 24. xiv. 25--35. But what just or satisfactory proof is there to be given why it ought to be believed that Satan tempts men by taking away the word out of the heart of those Jesus compared to the highway on which the seed was sown, lest they should believe and be saved, and yet not tempt or draw away those who have received the word with joy; and where, for a time, it promised fair for bringing forth fruit? For it is undeniable, that Jesus did not attribute it to the temptation of Satan, but to other manifest and common temptations to men, which cannot but be admitted, and which his hearers could easily understand; but, I presume, they could not, as it respected Satan as a fallen angel, for reasons and proofs already offered. The adversary to the several persons above represented, were the things of this world, such as Jesus mentioned, which too strongly operated upon the heart of some of them, as reasons why the word did not take any root in it: or why they did not accept of the invitation to the supper; and of others, who received it with joy, yet did not bring forth fruit to perfection; or, in the expressive words of Jesus, respecting the man who brought forth fruit, They had not an honest and good heart. The conduct of the men, compared to the seed sown by the highway, is affectingly exemplified in what is related of the young man, Mark x. 17--27. who asked Jesus what he should do to inherit eternal life? His riches, and the thought of parting with them as a condition thereto, made him go away without receiving the least benefit from the seed Jesus sowed in his heart. A parable similar with the foregoing is contained in v. 24--30. This Jesus explained to his disciples, v. 36--43. in which is contained these things; The field is the world, i. e. all men, both Jews and Gentiles, as v. 41. The seed sown represents the children of the kingdom, i. e. his disciples, called the righteous; v. 43, who are contradistinguished from the world, or the tares; or those who offend and do iniquity. The tares are descriptive of the latter persons, and are called the children of the wicked one, or the Devil, or the enemy who sowed tares among the wheat. The former are the good ground, which brought forth good fruit. If we were to interpret our Lord's words of the tares, literally, as the children of the wicked one, or the Devil, it would lead us to conclude it was wholly owing to his temptations and their influence, in causing them to offend and do iniquity, which cannot well be reconciled with, and admitted, by those who pay a proper attention to what he hath said of the causes or occasions of men being guilty of iniquity contained in these texts. Matt. xii. 34, &c. xv. 18, &c. xxiii. I. &c. Luke xi. 37, &c. Mark vii. 5, &c. Luke vi. 43, &c. John iii. 19, 20, 21. xii. 42, 43. In these passages it is very apparent that he attributes the wickedness, or iniquity of men to the influence which their different passions and inordinate desires have on their mind in producing their criminal dispositions and conduct, without giving the least intimation to those he addressed, that either or both arose from the temptations of the Devil, as an invisible apostate spirit. And similar with what he hath represented is that of the apostle, Rom. i. ii. iii. vi. respecting both Jews and Gentiles, who were all under sin, or they yielded their members, instruments of unrighteousness unto sin. This corrupt principle and conduct he calls the old man, which is corrupt, according to the deceitful lusts. Contrasted with the old man which they had put off, is the new man, which after God is created in righteousness and true holiness. The apostle personifies sin as the old man; but no rational man can well believe that he intended a real person, and that they had actually put him off or expelled him from them, but only that they had forsaken those sins which he stiles the old man. In like manner he is to be understood of the new man they had put on. From our Lord's words just quoted, and those of the Apostle, I think we may with an high degree of probability, at least conclude he did not intend a fallen angel, as the enemy, but the wicked conduct of ungodly men. The observations made upon the foregoing passages in Matthew, may possibly assist us in explaining another. John vii. 44. Jesus said to the Jews, ye are of your father the Devil, and the lusts of your father ye will do: he was a murderer from the beginning, and abode not in the truth, because there is no truth in him. When he speaketh a lie, he speaketh of his own, for he is a liar, and the father of it. In verse 34, he said, whosoever committeth sin is the servant of sin. In these words he personifies sin, calling it their master, and they his servants or slaves; in like manner as Paul represents the Romans before their conversion, chap. vi. He then changes the person to that of father, saying, Ye do that which ye have seen with your father; or, ye do the deeds of your father, v. 41. As he hath personified sin as their master, and also their father, whose deeds they did, from whence they became servants of the former, or children of the latter, by imitation. It surely cannot be judged to be offering violence to, or unjustifiably straining the sense of the word Devil, to suppose by that word he personified sin as their father, by doing his lusts, or deeds. I cannot well omit observing, that when the apostle mentioned Eve's transgression. 2. Cor. xi. 3. he did not say it was occasioned by the Devil's tempting her, but that it was by the subtilty of the serpent, as in Genesis. And it is undeniable that there is not one text in the Bible in which mention is made of her being tempted by the Devil; i. e. a fallen angel. That by their father, v. 38, Jesus did not mean the Devil, v. 44. seems pretty plain, from his saying, They did that which they had seen with their father. But, I presume, there is no man that believes they had seen the deeds of the Devil as a murderer and a liar. When Jesus represents the Jews he was speaking to as the children of the Devil, or that he was their father, he does not impute it to his secret viles or instigation in their hearts, no more than in verses 38. 41. After a like manner of expression he said to them, If ye were the children of Abraham ye would do the works of Abraham. But, I imagine, there is no man who believes he intended, that if they had done his works it would have been by the influence of his secret suggestions in their heart. But only that if they had heard and obeyed his word, like as Abraham did the

Revelations which God made to him, they would have been his children. See Rom. iv. 11, 12, 16. To the Jews Jesus said, Matt, xxiii. 31. Yet are witnesses to yourselves that ye are the children of them that killed the prophets. Or, as he faith, Luke xi. 48. Truly ye bear witness that ye allow the deeds of your fathers, for they indeed killed them, and ye build their sepulchres. But, I apprehend there is no man who believes that they were witnesses it was owing to the secret instigations or influence which those wicked men had on their minds which led them to act the part he accused them of; but his meaning is as in the other passage, that their principles and conduct were similar with those murderers of the prophets, and which the Jews afterwards manifested towards him, which he has described in the parable. Matt. xxi. 33. 38.[67]

---

[67] When in Acts xi, 9, 10, the Apostle characterizes Barjus as a child of the Devil, perhaps it is not easy to determine whether he intended that of sorcery alone, or included his other wicked principles and conduct he accused him of; or whether he attributes the latter as the effect of the former. If he intended that first mentioned, I presume it will be attended with insuperable difficulty in explaining how or after what manner an invisible spirit instructed him in the art of forcery, and the practice of it, so as for him to know that he received it from him. In the relation of the conversation which Peter had with Simon the sorcerer, chap. viii, he doth not give the least hint either that he was taught the art by the Devil, or that what he said to him of his heart not being right in the sight of God, and that he was in the gall of bitterness, and in the bond of iniquity, arose from the influence or power the Devil had over him. Yet, as these two characters are considerably similar, it is somewhat to be expected the Apostle would have attributed one or both to the same Being as Paul has done; I may just observe, that in every account we have in the Old Testament of sorcerers, and the kindred arts, there is not the least intimation that they received the knowledge of either from the Devil, or after what manner to practise them. If we suppose the Apostle Paul stiles Barjesus the Child of the Devil, on account of his being led or excited to commit those sins he accused him of, it may be replied that there is not any thing similar with it contained in the Old Testament, and yet those writings are the only authentic records from whence he could derive any knowledge of what

I would further observe, that as Jesus did not in any of the foregoing texts explain to his apostles or the Jews, his meaning of the word Satan, or the Devil, i. e. whether he was a fallen angel or not, they could not know he intended such a being, for reasons I have before offered; and, it is remarkable, that the text in John vii. 44. is the only one in which he attributed the principle and conduct of the unbelieving Jews towards himself to the Devil. For, in his numerous, severe, and pointed reproofs of them, he ascribed it to their corrupt hearts and wicked conduct, which they had too long manifested in their not keeping the law of God; or, as he tells them, had they believed Moses, they would have believed him; but, as they did not, they withstood the united and incontestible evidences he gave them, that he was the Son of God, and therefore they ought to obey his word. Must it not, therefore, to an attentive and unbiassed reader, appear somewhat difficult to be accounted for, that of those Jews only he has attributed their principle and conduct to the Devil; whereas, of all others, who were equally corrupt and unbelieving, he did not even once tell any of them they were his children, in the common acceptation of those words, especially when they gave him as great occasion for expressing himself in as pointed a manner. To instance only those Pharisees who wickedly and foolishly said he cast out devils, i. e. demons, by Belzebub the Prince of Devils, i. e. demons. As it is manifest our Saviour has personified the wicked Jews who killed the prophets, as the cause of producing children like themselves, i. e. the Jews he spake to, who, it is certain, had not the least influence in effecting it; why should it be judged

---

he mentions as the effect of the power of the Devil on the heart or actions of men. But if we may conclude that by the words Thou Child of the Devil, the Apostle intended only to express the enormity and complication of his crimes as a sorcerer and a very wicked immoral man, it will remove all the difficulty by giving an easy and rational solution of them. In like manner as I have shewn in what the Apostle John hath said of Cain, that he was of that wicked, or, as in the preceding verse, a Child of the Devil.

incredible that he should speak after a like manner in his using the words Satan, &c. The Apostle, in the 6th chapter to the Romans, has personified sin, as having been their lord and master, whom, before their conversion, they served, in fulfilling the desires of the flesh and of the mind. But every intelligent person, without the least objection, or difficulty, admits he is not to be understood in a literal sense, but only as an expressive figure, in which, in strong language, he describes their former wicked principles and conduct, as he doth in the 1st chapter.

Section 3

SECT. III. I have, in the foregoing pages, considered all the passages in the Evangelists, in which the wicked one, &c. is said to tempt men to sin; I will now attend to those in the Acts of the Apostles, and the other parts of the New Testament, of a similar kind.

AND the first that is related in the Acts, is chap. v. 3, 4, 9, concerning Ananias, to him Peter said, Why hath Satan filled thine heart to lie to the Holy Ghost, to keep back part of the price of the land?--After telling him, in the next verse, it was in his own power or choice to sell the land or not; and after he had sold it, to keep the price of it, or put it into the joint stock, he charged him with conceiving what he had done, saying, Why hast thou conceived this thing in thine heart? Thou hast not lied unto men, (in saying it was the whole given into the fund when it was but a part of it) but unto God. It may be said that Peter's words, v. 3, carry in them an affirmation that Ananias's heart was filled by Satan, as the moving or exciting cause of his committing that sin. Also that the Apostle really knew there was such a being, and that he temps men to sin. To which I reply, that the Apostle could not know either, from the Old Testament; and it is certain there is not any account in the Evangelists, that Jesus made any discovery of either to the Apostle, or other of them. And it is indisputably true, that he could not know either, by the light of his natural reason; besides, his attributing the sin to Satan, in the sense commonly understood, is not consistent with what he said to Ananias and his wife. To the former, Why hast thou conceived this thing in thine heart; thou hast not lied unto men, but unto God.--To the latter, How is it that we have agreed together to tempt the spirit of the Lord? In which he plainly attributes the primary moving cause to arise in their own breasts, and in contriving how they might put it in practice. Peter's words therefore may be thought to create some difficulty in determining whether he imputes Ananias's heart, being filled by Satan, or that the first rise of it was in himself, in conceiving the thing: for, if Peter believed it was primarily owing to the former, it could not be to the latter but only in a secondary sense; and had the Apostle known this to be the true state of the case, one would naturally conclude he would in one or both the latter addresses to him, have in that manner represented it: but, it is certain, from his own words, he hath not. From the whole relation of this singular transaction, it appears to me, that the primary excitement in the heart of Ananias, to contrive and put in execution what is related of him, arose from his own coveteous mind, which sugggested to him the thought of keeping back part of the price of the land, under the deluding hope, that could he succeed in concealing the transaction from the Apostle and others, he might receive from the joint stock a greater income than he had any right to; and also keep part of it for his own use; as may appear probable from chap. ii. 44, 45. iv. 32, 34, 35. and vi. 1, 2, 3. But their deceitful and criminal conduct was not only detected, but also punished of God, in a very signal and exemplary manner, as a solemn and affecting warning to other disciples, to avoid the like deceitful and wicked conduct.

That, by the word Satan, Peter did not intend a fallen angel, is to me undeniable from what I have observed of the entire silence in the Old Testament, of such a being, or his tempting men to sin, by his infusing evil thoughts into the mind; and that so far as we know, Jesus did not inform his Apostles of it. It follows therefore, that Ananias could not understand or believe that by the word Satan Peter intended such a being. Neither could Peter, so far as we know, have any real evidence on which to believe his heart was filled by him as the exciting cause of his doing what he did; or Ananias have any inward perception or consciousness of it. And, it hath been observed, that Peter imputes Ananias's sin to his conceiving the thing in his heart, and that he and his wife had agreed together in that act. When, in 2 Cor. xi. 14. the Apostle saith, Satan himself is transformed into an angel of light, I think he cannot well be understood to mean into one like an holy angel, it having no connection or coincidence with v. 13, 15. and therefore most probably he means an apostle of light, i.e. himself. See Gal. iv. 14. But then this transformation must be in a visible character, as a teacher of his tenets, or doctrines, or an invisible transformation. If we suppose the former to be his meaning it will be attended with very great, if not with insuperable difficulties, to account for; there not being the least hint, much less an instance of it related in the New Testament. If we suppose the Apostle means the latter, it will, I presume, be attended with equal difficulties. For, it is natural to ask, how, or by what means could his ministers come at the knowledge of this, or receive their doctrine, or any explicit direction or authority, as from him, or act as his ministers.

In the first Epistle chapter iv. 6. the same original word is translated I have--in a figure transferred--to myself, and Apollos--or rather to himself only; that is, I have contradistinguished, or contrasted myself and Apollos with the false apostles, for your sakes,, that as we always have acted as the stewards or servants of Christ only, and not made the least claim of headship over you, as though you were our disciples. (See chap. i. 12--15.) ye might learn, by our example, not to think of men, i. e. the false apostles, your leaders, above that which is written, and therefore not be puffed up for one against another. In this contrast of himself with the false apostles, he is not to be understood to admit their having the least claim to be the apostles of Christ any more than Satan, whom, he says, is transformed into an angel of light, i.e. an apostle of Christ. To the foregoing considerations I may add, that when the Apostles in his I Epistle i. ii. contrasts the tenets or doctrines of the false apostles with the revelations of the spirit of God made to him, or the wisdom of God in the gospel, which he had taught the Corinthians; he calls their wisdom the wisdom of the wise, the wisdom of men, and the wisdom and spirit of men, and the wisdom and spirit of the world, or of the Princes of this world; but he hath not given the least hint that it was the wisdom or doctrine of Satan, which had he belived, it is natural to conclude he would have mentioned it, as a very strong argument why they ought to renounce it, and the false apostles as his ministers; but of these things he is entirely silent. I will hazard a conjecture, and such I offer it, on v. 14, which, if admitted seems to obviate the difficulties above-mentioned, which is this, that one of the false apostles, on some account, perhaps as a Jew, chap i. 23. 2 Epistle xi. 22, 23, was head or chief among them, and on that account put himself upon an equality, in his apostolic character, with Paul, and that the others acted at least in a measure, if not wholly by his instruction and authority, and with him were deceitful workers transforming themselves into the apostles and ministers of Christ. The Apostles stiling him Satan, or an adversary, i. e. to him and his doctrine, is not much unlike what Jesus said of Peter, that he was Satan and of Judas, that he is a devil. When the Apostle, addressing himself to the Ephesians, Acts xx. 29. 30, saith, that after his departure, shall grievous wolves enter in among you, not sparing the flock, also of your own selves, shall men arise, speaking perverse things to draw away disciples after them, as was the conduct of those false apostles at Corinth, he doth not give them the least hint that any of them would be the ministers of Satan. And when our Saviour foretold that false teachers, or prophets, would arise and deceive many by their doctrine, he did not give the least intimation of their being the agents of Satan, or that they would receive his tenets, or act by his authority. The Apostle saith to the Ephesians, chap. ii. 2. That in times past ye walked according to the course of this world, according to the prince of the power of the air, the spirit that now worketh in the children of disobedience, among whom also we all had our conversation in times past in the lusts of the flesh and of the mind. Wheover reads Romans i, ii, iii, will plainly observe the Apostle hath given a particular and large representation of the principles and conduct of the Heathens, and in general from whence they arose; but it is certain he hath not attributed either to the temptations of Satan, but to the course of this world, or the examples of those they lived amongst, and from whom they learned them, by which they fulfilled the desires of the mind, &c. And the Apostle's representation of the principles and conduct of the Roman Christians before their conversion, as chap. vi.

perfectly corresponds with the above chapters. See also Ephes. iv. 17--22. Col. iii. 5--9. May we not therefore, with great probability, at least, if not with an absolute certainty, conclude, that by the Prince of the power of the air, the spirit that worked in the children of disobedience, the Apostle did not mean a fallen angel, but their own corrupt and wicked desires and principles; besides, it should be remembered it hath been shewed that there is not any account in the Old Testament, of a fallen angel, and therefore that neither Paul nor those Christians could know there was such a being, and that he tempted them to fulfil the desires of the mind, &c. Another text I will offer to the reader's consideration is Ephes. vi. 11, Put on the whole armour of God, that ye may be able to stand against the wiles of the Devil. Whoever believes that these Christians understood the Apostle, by the word Devil, to mean a fallen angel, and that they ought to stand against his wiles, left they should fail in acting agreeable to their Christian profession,--it will be natural to ask him from what unquestionable records or proofs they received the knowledge of each? That they did not, nor could receive it from the Old Testament, hath been made evident in the preceding pages. Also there is not the least trace in the Evangelists that Jesus revealed either to his disciples; and it is a certain truth that they could not know them from the light of nature, consequently they could not understand the Apostle in the sense generally embraced by men at this day. But if by the word Devil, the Apostle meant an adversary they were well acquainted with, it must mean men only who were their adversaries; and this appears to me evident from the next verse and verse 16. Compare Matt. x. 18. Mark xiii. 9, 12, 13, which perfectly accord with every expression of Jesus, in which he foretold to his disciples who would be their adversaries. See 1 Thess. iii. 3, 4, 5. And whoever reads Luke's History of the Acts, and Paul's writings, will plainly discern that it was such the Christians are exhorted to stand against their wiles. Besides, I may add, if they stood against, or resisted the wiles of an invisible spirit, which affected their minds as a temptation, they must not only evidently perceive its operation and influence on their mind, but also distinguish those wiles from other excitements of temptation, arising either within themselves or from the impression of external causes. But I am fully convinced that there are no proofs or facts in Scripture to evince that they or any others did make such a distinction between them; and yet if they did not, I leave it to the consideration of the impartial enquirer to explain clearly the means by which they could really know what were his wiles, and also when they stood against or resisted them. It is upon their being able to make this distinction that they could discern and form a true judgment of the propriety and applicableness of the Apostle's exhortation to them. The foregoing observations, I apprehend, may tend to explain our Lord's words to Paul, Acts xxvi. 18, that he sent him to the Gentiles to turn them from darkness to light, and from the power of Satan, unto God. See v. 20. I should think it can hardly be doubted, that by the Gentiles being in darkness, and in the power of Satan, are designed to express the same thing, and not that the former was the effect of the power of the latter. After a like manner I presume we are to understand the words turned to light, or unto God, are expressive of the same state, i. e. their conversion to the gospel. Ephes. iv. 20--24. Now, what the state of darkness is, or the sins intended, we learn from Rom. xiii. 12, 13, 14. The Apostle, writing to the Gentile Colossians, useth expressions perfectly equivalent with those we are considering, I. 13. Who hath delivered us from the power of darkness, and hath translated us into the kingdom of his dear Son. What he intends by their having been in the power of darkness, i. e. their former sins, is plain from iii. 1--8. and Ephes. iv. 17--19. v. 8, 11, 12. Another text, somewhat similar with that in Ephesians ii. 2. already considered, is what the Apostle saith, 2 Cor. iv. 4. In whom the God of this world hath blinded the minds of them that believe not, lest the light of the glorious gospel of Christ, who is the image of God, should shine unto them.[68] By comparing these

---

[68] Sir Edward Knatchbull in his Annotations, renders the words under consideration thus:--"If our gospel be hid, it is hid among those that are lost; among whom God hath blinded the minds of the unbelievers of

words with chapter the 3d, and particularly with verses 13, 14, 15, it appears very plain to me, that he spake of the unbelieving Jews respecting their blindness of mind, i. e. they did not see the true design and end of the law as centering in Christ, no more than the Israelites saw the face of Moses when he covered it with a veil. That by the God of this world, the Apostle did intend Satan, and that he was the real cause of the blindness of mind of the Jews, is plain to me from his own account of it in these texts. Rom. ix. 31, 32, 33. x. 1--4. xi. 7--32. I Cor. i. 22, 23. See also I Pet. ii. 7, 8, John ix. 39, 40, 41. Matt. xiii. 13, 14, 15. And the Apostle himself was a remarkable instance of that blindness of mind, or his ignorance in unbelief, which he imputed to the Jews. But, I judge, it will appear evident to every one who is conversant in his writings, that he hath not even once attributed it to Satan as the god of this world, but to other causes, as manifest facts, from whence it arose. I Tim. i. 13. Neither hath Jesus, nor the Evangelists, in any one text, ascribed the blindness of mind of the Jews, to the God of this world, i. e. to Satan; but to very different ones that are plainly related in their writings, and therefore are easily discerned and admitted by every impartial reader.

The Apostle Peter, in his 1st epistle, v. 8, 9, 10, faith, Be sober, be vigilant, because your adversary the Devil, as a roaring lion, walketh about seeking whom he may devour, whom resist

---

this age, lest the light of the glorious gospel of Christ should shine unto them (that is so shine) as that they should see and understand." See Rom. xi. 3, &c. 2, Thes. ii. 10, 11, 12. If the Apostle alluded to Isaiah vi. 8, &c. it is plain that their hearing and not understanding, &c. is represented as from God, who sent him to deliver that message to them. For though it is said in John xii 39, 40, Therefore they (that is the Jews, to whom Jesus addressed himself) could not believe, because that Esaias said again, &c. Yet I presume it cannot reasonably be believed that the prophet of himself was able to effect what is mentioned. The true reason or cause of their hearing and not understanding, &c. was their wicked principles and conduct, as appears plain from Isaiah chap. i. Jer. v. 21. Ezek. xii. 2. And in a like sense is Paul to be understood, Acts xxviii. 24--27.

stedfast in the faith, knowing that the same afflictions are accomplished in your brethren that are in the world. But the God of all grace, who hath called us to his eternal kingdom, by Jesus Christ, after that ye have suffered a while, (i.e. under those afflictions) make you perfect, establish, strengthen, settle you. This representation of the Devil, or adversary (they are exhorted to resist) in his eagerness after, and devouring his prey, or whom he may, is manifestly taken from the lion's ravenous fierceness after his prey; and when he has seized it, his devouring it. And whoever reads the following texts, besides many more, will plainly discern it fully exemplified in the persecutors of the disciples of Jesus, especially by the unbelieving Jews, in their ravenous spirit and conduct towards them. Acts viii. 13, 21. Gal. i. 13. Acts xiii. 44, 45, 50. xvi. 5, 6, 7, 13. xxi. 27--31. xxii. 21, 22, 23. xxiii. 12, &c. I Cor. xi. 24, 25. But the Apostle's representation does not equally, if at all, apply to the conduct of the Devil, who, by most men, is supposed to attack men by his secret or imperceptible devices, or instigations on their mind or heart. Even his tempting Jesus, as it is related, doth not accord with Peter's representation. I think it is natural to suppose, that the afflictions which these Christians endured, and were accomplished, also in their brethren that were in the world, from the same kind of adversary, are the persecutions the Apostle mentions more at large, chap. iii. 12--19. If this is admitted, as most probable, we cannot well fail in understanding him to mean the adversary that persecuted them. Perhaps to this will be objected his exhorting them to resist the adversary as though he intended a personal resistance. But to this it may be replied, in his own words; it was by being stedfast in the faith, i. e. by an inflexible adherence to their profession as Christians. There are two texts in which the same original word occurs, that may serve to illustrate and confirm this to be his meaning. Our Saviour told his Apostles, Luke xxi. 15, I will give you a mouth and wisdom, which all your adversaries shall not be able to resift. This was exemplified in Stephen, Acts vi. 9. 10. The unbelieving Jews were not able to resist the wisdom and the spirit by which he spake to them. In this case there was resisting on both sides; on his it was by the wisdom and the spirit. To those Peter wrote to there was no difficulty in their knowing what were their own afflictions and those of their brethren that were in the world, but there seems to me a very considerable one attending their knowing what they were, if understood, of the wiles or devices of an invisible spirit on their hearts or minds. Should it be said that the Devil stirred up or excited their enemies to persecute them, and in that sense he exhorted them to resist him; I answer, that in the many texts in the Evangelists in which Jesus declared to his apostles and disciples what it was that would stir up their enemies to persecute them, he has not even once attributed it to the Devil. Neither hath Luke, in his History of the Apostles, in describing the persecutions they met with, even in one text, attributed it to him. Instead of this, Jesus and that historian have ascribed it to other and very different causes that are therein plainly related, and very much because they were his disciples; or, as he said, If they persecute me, they will also persecute you. There is one text in the I Epistle to the Thessalonians, that, I judge, will illustrate and confirm the foregoing explication of that under consideration, chap. ii. 18. Wherefore we would have come unto you (even I, Paul) once and again, but Satan hindered us. In looking into Acts xvii. it appears, that after he had converted many of the Thessalonians to the faith of Christ, or that they had obeyed the gospel he preached to them, the unbelieving Jews seeing his success, stirred up the baser sort of the people, and raised so great a persecution against him, and the new converts, that the brethren judged it expedient to send away Paul by night, in a secret manner, who went to Berea, where, for some time, he preached the gospel, and converted many of them. Upon those Jews at Thessalonica, hearing of this, they came there also, and acted after a like manner; upon which account the brethren sent Paul away to Athens, some of whom accompanied him, but Timothy and Silas continued behind. In this state of things the Apostle left his new converts at Thessalonica, at which his mind was so uneasy, that when Timothy came to him at Athens, he sent him back to them, that he might comfort and establish them in their faith under their persecutions; who, on his return to Corinth, Acts xviii. 5. brought him a most agreeable account of their stedfastness in the faith. On a view of this state of things, there seems to be great difficulty in judging who the Satan, or adversary is, that hindered him from returning to them, as he had more than once wished to do, namely, the persecuting Jews. That which adds some force to this explication, is, what he says, chap. iii. 4, 5, 6. For, verily, when we were with you we told you before, that we should suffer tribulation, even as it came to pass, and ye know, for this cause, when I could no longer forbear, I sent to know your faith, left, by some means, the tempter having tempted you, and our labour be in vain, &c. The tempter likely to tempt them, appears evident from the context, i. e. the persecuting Jews, by whom they suffered tribulation, as well as himself. The Apostle James, in chap. iv. 7. faith, resist the Devil, and he will flee from you. In verses 5, 6, he tells them, The spirit, or temper that dwells in some of them, lusteth to envy. But to those who endeavoured to govern it, he assures them for their encouragement, that God giveth more grace, but he resisteth the proud and envious, but giveth grace unto the humble. And then he very justly exhorts them to submit themselves to God, i. e. to his grace; resist the Devil and he will flee from you. Draw nigh to God, and he will draw night to you. If, by their resisting the Devil, the Apostle means the spirit of pride and envy excited or stirred up in them by him; or that by his secret influence he strengthened it, than for the persons to judge of the propriety and justness of his exhortation, they must have clear evidence by which they could know it was really produced or wrought in them by the Devil, unless the Apostle and the persons believed it never existed in the minds of men, but from that cause alone; which, I presume, no one will attempt to prove, much less effect it. For if it is allowed, as surely it will, that the spirit of pride may be, and is often produced in the mind of man, from very different causes, both internal as well as external. If this is allowed, then the person in whom it dwells, must, as was observed, have a real inward perception, or evidence, by which he can and actually did distinguish its arising from the excitation or influence of the Devil, and not from other and very different causes, otherwise he would not have been able to know, with any real certainty, it arose from him. For if he is incapable of making that distinction, he certainly cannot know whether he resists the Devil, or any internal or outward well known cause, or causes, from whence that spirit lusting in him, may be, or is produced; and when not resisted, shews itself in envy to others. And, I persuade myself, there is not now any rational man who believes that Satan does tempt men to be proud, or envious, that can make that distinction, or discrimination between that which is excited in him by Satan, and what arises from his natural passion not duly governed, and from whence he is drawn into sin. This pride and envy the Apostle speaks of, seems, from the context, to be the adversary they were to resist, and concerning which they were competent judges; but, I apprehend, they were not, as it respected an invisible spirit. Indeed, did it appear that the sacred writers have always, or very generally attributed pride, or the usual effect of it, envy, to the secret instigation of the Devil, as a fallen angel, there would be some reason to believe that the Apostle intended him in the text under consideration; but, I presume, it will not be found thus represented in any of those writings. Similar with the Apostle's words, are those of Paul, Ephes. iv. 29, 27, Be ye angry and sin not; let not the sun go down upon your wrath, neither give place to the Devil. The above observation, I judge, will apply equally to these words, because no one can really distinguish between anger and its effects, as arising from any external cause, affecting that passion, and what may be effected in him by the influence of an invisible spirit. In chap. i. 14, 15, the Apostle hath given a very plain account of what are the inward natural causes in every man, of his being tempted, i. e. when he is drawn away of his own lust, and enticed. Then when lust hath conceived, it bringeth forth sin. This is so entirely correspondent to the natural and universal experience of every man, that I should judge it will be admitted is not only justly founded, but so far as men really know what passes within themselves, is the original, inward, and true cause of their being tempted to sin. The Apostle John, in his I Epistle iii. 8. 10, faith, He that committeth sin is of the Devil, for the Devil sinneth from the beginning. For this purpose the Son of God was manifested that he might destroy the works of the Devil. In this the children of God are manifest, and the children of the Devil. Whoever doth not righteousness is not of God, neither he that loveth not his brother. Understanding these words literally and without limitation, and comparing them with chap. v. 18, 19, some may be ready to suppose he believed and has asserted, that every wicked action men commit, originates from the influence or devices of the Devil in their heart, and that Jesus was sent to destroy his power in them, or his work manifest in their conduct. The Apostle saith of Cain, verse 12, he was of that wicked one, or one of the children of the Devil; as v. 10. who slew his brother, or did not love him, and wherefore slew he him, because his own works were evil, and his brother's righteous. These words may assist us in explaining those under consideration, and the last cited text; for he himself has here assigned the real and true cause from whence Cain was excited to commit that wicked action. And this perfectly agrees with what is related in Gen. iv. 4, &c. where it is said, The Lord had respect unto Abel, and to his offering; but unto Cain and his offering he had not respect, and Cain was very wrath, and his countenance fell. To whom the Lord said, Why art thou wrath, and why is thy countenance fallen? If thou dost well shalt thou not be accepted; and if thou dost not well, sin lieth at the door. Under this state of Cain's mind, and his suffering his wrath to overcome his reason, and his not being influenced by what the Lord said to him, it is manifest be was excited to kill his brother; or, in the words of the Apostle James, just cited, He was tempted being drawn away by his own lust, and enticed; and when lust had conceived, it brought forth sin. In the above chapter it is indisputable that there is not the least intimation of Cain's being tempted to that action by the instigation of the Devil, as a fallen angel, as was noted. The Apostle hath assigned the true cause of his slaying his brother, which coincides with what is related in

Genesis. Seeing then he speaks of Cain as of that wicked one, or one of the children of the Devil, though it doth in the last appear from Genesis, nor his own words, that he was excited to it by him, but by his own wrath against his brother. Why should it be believed he attributes his sin, or that of all other men, to the wicked one, or the Devil. By either of those words one would therefore rather be led to believe the Apostle intends an adverfary like as was that to Cain, i. e. mens unsubdued passions, or desires; and on that account he calls them the children of the Devil, or of the wicked one; and from mens having been influenced there-by, the world laid in wickedness, correspondent to which the Apostle speaks of the Gentile world, Ephef. v. 6. Col. iii. 6. That they were the childred of disobedience. Or to the Thessalonians, they were children of the night, and of darkness; or, in our Lord's words to the unbelieving Jews, That they were the children of those men who in ages past killed the prophets. Compare what hath been observed with Rom. vi. in which chapter the Apostle attributes the wickedness of the Heathen world to a like adverfary that led Cain to slay his brother, i. e. they yielded their members or passions as instruments of unrighteousness unto sin; or by obeying the lusts of their mortal body, sin reigned in and over them. To reform men from their sins which arose from those causes, as their adversary was one of the primary ends and purposes for which the Son of God was manifested that he might destroy those works; or, in the words of the Apostle John, the works of the Devil. That which will much illustrate what I have observed, are the exhortations of the Apostle Paul to those in whom Christ, by his ministers, had destroyed their wicked works. And the whole of it is comprehended in the last cited chapter. To whom he faith, Let not sin reign in your mortal body, that ye should obey it in the lusts thereof, &c. and add, Ephef. v. 25, 26, 27. iv. 17--29. v. 3, &c. Col. iii. 5--10. In further support and illustration of the fore-going scripture proofs and observations, shewing it is at least highly probable, if not absolutely certain, that the passages I have quoted, are not to be understood, in the common acceptation, of the real existence of a fallen angel, and that he tempts men to sin, I will offer what the Apostle faith, Gal. iv. 17. Rom. vii. 21, 22, 23, compared with vi. II--20.

In chap. vii. he clearly describes the Jews as sinners under the law, wherein it is exceeding evident to me, he represents the inward man as consisting of two parts; one is, his reason and conscience; the other, his several passions and appetites. The former are appointed by the Author of his being, to rule or govern the latter; and when they are not under its direction and control, they move and excite him to sinful actions, in opposition to his reason and conscience. And he as plainly describes the inward struggle, or conflict between them; one as the law of his mind, and the other the law of his members; and that when the latter prevails over the former, he is brought into captivity to sin; or, in his own words, I find then a law, that when I would do good, evil is present with me; or, I see a law in my members warring against the law of my mind, and bringing me into captivity to the law of sin, which is in my members; or, as he expresses it in other words in the Galatians, The flesh lusteth against the spirit, and the spirit against the flesh; and these are contrary the one to the other, so that ye do not the things that ye would. The lusts of the flesh are particularly mentioned, Rom. i, 19, &c. Gal. v. 19, 20, 21. I cannot avoid particularly observing, that in the fore-cited chapters the Apostle hath not even hinted that the members of the man who is captivated by sin, is excited or stirred up, or brought into that state by Satan, but entirely by his own ungoverned lusts, or inordinate desires warring against the law of his mind. And yet, I should think, it will be allowed to be natural to expect he would have mentioned this with the other causes of it, especially considering what he has particularly said upon that subject, had he been of the same opinion with most men at this day, who attribute almost, if not all the sins which men commit, to the devices of Satan. I shall here subjoin Mr. Farmer's explication of some texts where the words Devil and Satan occur, and I will here produce several passages from the New Testament:--Have not I (saith Christ) chosen you twelve, and one of you is a Devil?--He here refers to the traitor, who was not the chief of fallen angels, but one who acted the part of an enemy in betraying his master. Neither give place to the Devil; that is, give no occasion to the railer or slanderer to reproach your religion; which is the sense given of this passage by Erasmus and others. A Bishop must not be a novice, or a new convert, left, being lifted up with pride, he falls into the condemnation of the Devil, or calumniator. Moreover he must have a good report of them that are without, lest he should fall into reproach, and the snare of the Devil, or the adversary and the slanderer. It is hard to say what peculiar advantage the Devil might derive from a Bishop's want of a good report of them that are without; but it is easy to see that this would expose him to the censure and to the stratagems of the enemies of religion, who might try to shame him out of those principles, which served only to reproach and condemn him. The term Devil, is used in the plural number, in the New Testament, just as Satan is in the Old; when it cannot refer to fallen angels. St. Paul, in two of his epistles, forbids women to be Devils, rendered slanderers, and false accusers. I Tim. iii. 11. Titus ii. 3. In this sense it is used of men, 2 Tim, iii. 3, and rendered false accusers. In the I Epistle to the Corinthians, chap. v. 5, are these words respecting the incestuous member of that congregation:--To deliver such an one unto Satan for the destruction of the flesh, that the spirit may be saved in the day of the Lord Jesus. To an attentive and unbiassed man who reads thess words and the context, I believe he will find it extremely difficult to form a just conception in what sense the person was to be delivered unto, or put in the power of Satan, if understood to be an invisible spirit, especially to answer the end there mentioned; for it cannot consistent with reason be supposed, much less believed, that a malevolent spirit, being the avowed enemy of man, as is generally believed he is, would exert his power over him, to effect that salutary end; but on the contrary, try his utmost to continue his impenitence perpetual, that he might not be saved. If we may be permitted to suppose, that by his being delivered unto Satan, means not only his being separated from the congregation, equally as he was before his conversion;

but also excluded from the benefits he enjoyed as a member of Christ's body; and that this would have a very probable tendency to bring him to a true sense of his crime, that he might be saved. It will, I presume, be the most natural and rational explication of the Apostle's general meaning, and which seems to be confirmed from the effect it produced, as mentioned by him, 2 Ephes, ii. 5, &c. vii. 12. Somewhat similar to the incestuous Corinthian being delivered unto Satan, &c. is what the Apostle mentions, 1 Tim. iii. 20, of his conduct towards Hymencus and Alexander, whom he had delivered unto Satan, that they might learn not to blaspheme. But can any rational man really believe, that if they had been delivered into the power of a malignant spirit, the supposed enemy of man, that he would have exerted it to reform them from their wicked conduct, that they might not in future blaspheme, but act consistent with their Christian character?--I presume he cannot believe this of him, but, on the contrary, that he would have exerted his influence over them to continue it. Whatever therefore the Apostle meant by the word Satan, he cannot in reason be understood to intend a malignant apostate angelic spirit. Should any one suppose that by delivering either of the persons unto Satan, the Apostle intends his inflicting on them some bodily or mental disorder, by which means the former might be saved in the day of the Lord Jesus, and the latter persons learn thereby not to blaspheme; it may be justly replied, that such a supposition hath not the least countenance or support from any thing of the kind in all the Bible, and therefore is inadmissible in explaining the genuine meaning of the Apostle. Should it be urged that the bodily and mental disorders which the Demoniacs were afflicted with, related in the Evangelists, were inflicted by the Devil, as a fallen angel, it may be justly replied, that they are not attributed to such a being, but to a demon or demons, i. e. the soul or spirit of man departed. For in every instance which in our translation the word Devil or Devils, is rendered Diamonion and not Diabolos. In reference to this very case of the offender, the Apostle saith to his brethren, chap. ii. 10, 11, that he forgave him upon his repentance in the person, or by the authority of Christ, and that the brethren ought to do the like, for which he assigns this reason, viz. Lest Satan get an advantage of us, for we are not ignorant of his devices. If the Apostle and his brethren were not ignorant, but really knew what they were; or as the original word is rendered the mind, as chap. iii. 24. iv. 4. xi. 3. of Satan; it is certain they were better qualified to prevent his getting an advantage of them, than all other men who have not that knowledge of his devices; but if they really had that knowledge of them, it is natural to ask from whence or by what means they obtained it, for it is certain that they could not, from any part of the Old Testament writings, know not that there is such a being as a fallen angel, as I have made appear. By Satan, or the enemy, I think it probable the Apostle means the enemies of the Christian religion, who might take advantage by refusing to receive the penitent offender again into their fellowship, by representing them as rigorously inflexible in their conduct towards them. Should it be objected that the Apostle useth the word Satan in the singular, and therefore that my explication of many enemies doth not accord there-with; I answer, so he does of the word Satan and Tempter, in I Thess. ii. 18 iii. 5. But I have shewed it to be at least very probable that he means the Jews who were his and their enemies. Since the publication of this Tract, it hath been objected that the opinion therein maintained is injurious to practical religion, by inducing men to believe that they have no other enemy to encounter with, but what arises from themselves and the snares of the world;--I know of no better answer to it, than the Apostle James hath given, in the words already cited. That every man is tempted when he is drawn away of his own lust and enticed, &c. See Matt. xiii. 21, 22, 23. Mark iv. 17, 18, 19. And this is unquestionably confirmed from the experience of every sinner, at this time, and in all past ages, and also from the testimony of all history, both sacred and prophane.

Conclusion

IF the explanation of the passages quoted in the preceding pages, are justly founded and admitted, it will have an immediate and happy tendency to relieve the minds of those who believe, that at certain times they are conflicting with the secret and evil suggestions of Satan, and the influence they judge they have upon their heart, as what occasions much disquietude and perplexity, and interrupts their peace; and in some persons this is very considerable. To those who may see just reason to be of the same opinion with the writer, will plainly see, that much of the subject of sermonizing is not sounded in scripture, but arises from mistaking, or not clearly understanding the genuine meaning of those writers on the subject here discussed. To shew men in the clearest manner by what means, or from what real and apparent causes they are liable to, or are tempted to sin, which they themselves are capable of perceiving with certainty, from what passes within them, or their own inward feeling or experience; or that every man is tempted when he is drawn away of his own lust and enticed; and that lust when it hath conceived, bringeth forth sin, will certainly have a plain and direct tendency to warn them against it; and if thereby they are drawn into sin, by what means they may deliver themselves out of it, i.e. by over-ruling or subduing their lusts, or evil desires for the future. But to exhort men to resist a tempter, whose suggestions or devices on their hearts, they are not able to distinguish from their own evil lusts or desires, must, I presume, appear to every rational man, but of little practical use; whereas that which was just mentioned they perfectly well know, because it is grounded upon almost every day's experience in themselves and in others. In the foregoing pages I have offered to the reader's consideration every material passage in the New Testament, where in general or particular is related the devices or temptations of the Devil, &c. with my observations and explications of them. As I am convinced, they run counter to the very general and long established opinion which men of every denomination have of Satan, &c. and of his tempting men to sin, I must beg a truce with such persons, requesting that with as little bias and prejudice as they are capable of, they will examine the several texts I have offered, and the contexts, and weigh the evidence on which they have been explained, as what appears to me to be their genuine import; and I would hope that the sensible and discerning part of my readers will not suffer themselves to be influenced and governed in their judgment by the antiquity of their opinion, or, because it has been sanctioned by many men of distinguished learning and abilities, who, in their annotations on those passages, have given a very different sense of them than I have offered.[69]

There is one opinion respecting Satan, or the Devil, that in this enlightened age is very much, if not entirely relinquished, which, for many ages past was universally, or at least very generally believed to be founded upon the testimony of scripture; and that is his bewitching men, by having possession in them, or, at least, by his secret influence on their mind. And were men as calmly and with a like unprejudiced mind, to attend to the texts already cited, and the explication given of them, it is probable they will see just reason to alter their opinion of his tempting men to sin; as what appears to me is alike unsounded in those writings. At least, in reading these pages, it is possible they may discern clearer and stronger proofs on the opposite sides of the question, than they apprehend could be offered in favor of it. Should the foregoing explication of the passages which represent Satan as a tempter of men to sin, appear to be the true meaning of them, I presume it will tend to remove an objection which some persons may make against Revelation, or those parts of it. For, I should judge, it will be allowed, at least, by many persons, that exclusive

---

[69] The veneration that men have for writings of great name and eminent piety, incline them to admit all their opinions at once, without examination; on the other hand they reject, without hesitation, the doctrines proposed to them by those who are censured as impious and prophane; Fearing to partake of other mens guilt, they dread conviction as a crime. FARMER.

of such a tempter, or that men derive any moral corruption from the sin of their first parents, they are of themselves too much inclined or prone to transgress the law of their nature and the precepts of Revelation. For to suppose that they are under the power or influence of those two additional excitements to it, must lay such a strong bias upon their rational powers, or the law of the mind, in their choosing or willing what is right and their duty to perform, as cannot but place them in a state exceedingly disadvantageous to their moral and religious improvement, especially those of them who have not the advantage of knowing the precepts and motives contained in Revelation; and which, if admitted, may be found not reconcileable with the goodness of God, their Creator.[70] That man is liable to be tempted to sin by his own passions, or inordinate desires, when they are not properly governed, exclusive of any moral taint or corruption, he is by many supposed to derive from the sin of his first parents, is undeniable from their first transgression; who, it is certain, were not from thence in the least excited or influenced to transgress against the positive law of God given them. If the explication I have given of the texts cited in the preceding pages, be justly founded, it is possible the following objection may be made to it, which is, How, or by what means are we to account for what Jesus, the Evangelist, and the Apostles have said of Satan or the Devil, as a being then existing, if there really be no such being? For, it will be urged, that what they have said of his acts, implies it; and also their exhortations to resist his devices and temptations.--To which I answer, if there be any force in the objection, it equally applies to what they have said of Demons, which, in a like manner supposes not only their existence, but also

---

[70] I submit it to the deliberate judgment of the intelligent and enlightened reader, whether the belief of Satan's being the principal if not the sole cause of mens sinning, and consequently of the effects resulting from it are not too coincident with and patronizes the Manichian opinion of an evil principle to be admitted by those who profess the Christian religion, which plainly teaches them that God alone rules and governs over all his mortal creatures.

their having power to possess the bodies of men, and produce disorders in them, such as are related in the New Testament; and yet, notwithstanding this, I presume it is a truth not to be disproved or justly controverted, that neither the Evangelists, nor the Apostles had, or could have received any real knowledge of either of those things; and for these unanswerable reasons, viz. Because there is not any revelation made of them in the Old Testament; and it is impossible by the light of their natural reason, or understanding, they could derive any knowledge of them, any more than it respects Satan, and for the same reasons. And there is not the least account in the New Testament that Jesus revealed those things to the Apostles or Evangelists. To me it appears, that the only obvious method of answering the objection, or accounting for what those persons have mentioned of demons is, by admitting the disorders or infirmities of mens bodies to be natural indispositions, and not the effects of a possessing demon, or an human departed spirit. So likewise what they have said of Satan and his acts, may, on a like ground, be considered as the lusts or evil desires of men, excited in them from various causes, by which, as the Apostle James saith, every man is tempted when he is drawn away of his own lust, and enticed; and when lust hath conceived, it bringeth forth sin. I readily own, that were there any clear revelation, in the Old Testament, of a fallen angel, and that he tempted men to sin, it would certainly be very natural to understand the several texts I have cited, in the common acceptation of them; but, as I have just observed, there is not in those writings any mention of either of those particulars. If the foregoing proofs, from Scripture, and the observations founded thereon, are admitted, as entirely invalidating the common opinion concerning the Devil, or Satan, and his tempting men to sin, it eventually and decidedly proves that the Heathen oracles and the Priests and Priestesses being inspired by such a being, is entirely groundless, there being not the least proof of their reality; but they wholly originated from, and were supported by the cunning and artful. Whether the learned or unlearned, or both, who were concerned therein, and who, therefore, whether from sinister or political ends, or both, imposed on the weakness and credulity of the people. And these observations, and the conclusion just mentioned, are equally true, as it respects demons, i. e. the souls of men departed, whether of heroes or others.

POSTSCRIPT.

If the foregoing proofs, from Scripture, and the reasoning deduced from them, that there is not any real evidence of there being any fallen angel, or angels; and that they tempt men to sin, is justly founded, it will eventually and decidedly prove, that no man in any past age of the world, hath been possessed by one of them; and, consequently, that any bodily or mental disorders, or both, that have, by Dr. Worthington and others, been ascribed to their power in, or over men, is wholly void of any evident or real proof from Scripture; and consequently, that the testimony of the Fathers in the primitive ages, or by any other writers in more modern ones, have not any real foundation in truth, notwithstanding the very circumstantial relations they gave of them, and consequently, that the many accounts which those writers give of the manner or the means by which they have asserted that such a spirit, or spirits were expelled or cast out of the bodies of men, cannot be admitted, but must be attributed to the mistaken opinion they had concerning such a being, and his power over men; and therefore, that in those relations there is not any real evidence or proof for the truth of the Christian religion; however they were then and have since been urged to that purpose even in this age. In asserting and maintaining what I have just mentioned, as what appears to me is built upon unquestionable evidence, I know I differ very much from men of high repute for their great learning and abilities, who have been, and still are advocates for the contrary opinion. Whatever credit is justly due to the writings of the Fathers as it respects their account of real transactions which then took place, and of which they were competent to judge, and in recording which, their minds were not influenced by any strong religious prejudices of education, may be admitted; yet, in the cases we have mentioned, there is, in my opinion, just ground to disbelieve them, as what neither Scripture nor any real facts evince the truth of. To urge, that some of the Fathers, and other writers since, were men of great abilities and learning, as well as of integrity, which I do not deny, and therefore that they were competent to judge in such cases as we are mentioning, is not, in my opinion, a sufficient security against their being mistaken concerning them, as not visible to their notice and inspection, and in which they were liable to be misguided in their judgment by the strength of rooted prejudices, not only from education, but by the concurring sentiments of many others their cotemporaries.

FINIS

www.ingramcontent.com/pod-product-compliance
Lightning Source LLC
Chambersburg PA
CBHW072200100426
42738CB00011BA/2488